BROTHERS AND RIVALS: PATRILOCALITY IN SAVAGE COVE

Melvin M. Firestone

Newfoundland Social and Economic Studies No. 5
Institute of Social and Economic Research
Memorial University of Newfoundland
St. John's, Newfoundland
1967

ACKNOWLEDGEMENTS

This study was part of a research programme commissioned under the
Agricultural Rehabilitation and Development Act (Statutes of Canada,
1960/1961: Chapter 30). The Institute gratefully acknowledges this
sponsorship.

First, I would like to thank the members of my dissertation
committee, Drs. Viola Garfield, Simon Ottenberg, Kenneth Read, Edgar
Winans, and James B. Watson for their guidance and recommendations.
Dr. Watson is to be particularly thanked for his patience in his more
than ten year tenure as my committee head. I owe a great deal to Dr.
Melford Spiro, now of the University of Chicago, for his intellectual
stimulation and theoretical framework.

My thanks go to the Institute of Social and Economic Research
of Memorial University for providing me with a two year fellowship,
from 1963 to 1965, when the field work was carried on and most of the
dissertation written. I want to thank Dr. Ian Whittaker, then of the
Institute, for selecting me as a fellow and for his guidance during
my field work. Dr. Herbert Halpert, of the English Department at
Memorial, encouraged my culture-historical inclinations, and Dr. Nels
Anderson, of the Department of Sociology and Anthropology, read and
aptly criticized much of the text. I am also indebted to the following
faculty members at Memorial University for their aid and interest:
Dr. Leslie Harris of the Department of History, Dr. Allan Williams,
then of the Department of Geography, Drs. E. R. Seary and William Kirwin
of the Department of English, and Mr. Hugh Lilly of the Department of
Geology.

My fellow research fellows who have worked in other parts of
Newfoundland and Labrador and who have provided me with valuable
comparative information and insights are: Shmuel Ben-Dor, Louis
Chiaramonte, James Faris, Tom Philbrook, and John Szwed.

In the Strait of Belle Isle my thanks go to Rev. and Mrs. Jacob
Rogers and Rev. Arthur Churchill of Flower's Cove for their council,
and to Mr. and Mrs. Howard Genge of Flower's Cove for their hospitality.
The staffs of the International Grenfell Association Nursing Station

at Flower's Cove and Hospital at St. Anthony have indebted myself and
my wife to them for various kindnesses. In particular I would like to
thank nurses Audry Plint and Catherine Roy, and Drs. Alisstar Smith
and John Stutzman. Only Miss Plint is at present with the International
Grenfell Association.

I cannot begin to express my thanks to the people of Savage Cove
and the Strait of Belle Isle. I could not mention any person in Savage
Cove without slighting another. My wife and I were treated with such
courtesy, hospitality, and warmth as to make us feel Savage Cove our
second home.

CONTENTS

I must begin with an apology to the people of Savage Cove. They were
not consulted as to whether they cared to be descended upon by an
anthropologist, but they endured his prying cheerfully and with
interest. I must perhaps also apologize for not changing the name
of the community—Savage Cove is not a pseudonym. I have retained the
name for various reasons. First, I have discussed toponymy and social
history in the Strait of Belle Isle and it is not possible to do this
accurately unless real names are used. Second, the actual community
studied, is of course, general knowledge in the area and so there
would be no doubt locally as to which settlement reference was being
made. Since emotional involvement is parochial I see no need to hide
the name of the community from strangers who have no commitment towards
it. Finally, I have the feeling, which I cannot substantiate, that
the people of Savage Cove would be disappointed if I changed the name.

In order to present as much as possible of the local view of
things I have in some places quoted actual phrases or sentences spoken
by members of the community. The sources of these are, of course, not
given. Such utterances appear surrounded by quotation marks or as
indented paragraphs. I have presented local terms for the above reason
and also so they may be noticed by the student of Newfoundland speech.

If I have included more details of local culture than are needed
to illustrate local social structure it is in the hope that they will
help provide a needed record of a rapidly changing folk tradition.

Although this is the study of a particular community what I
have to say about it generally pertains to the Newfoundland side of
the Strait of Belle Isle. I was not able to do extensive work in
other communities, for I was in the area but the total of one year
(from October, 1963 to August, 1964, and during June, 1965), but it
was sufficient to give me the strong impression that Savage Cove is
fairly representative of the region.

There are, however, differences in the character of the various
communities: differences in aggressiveness, sobriety, fear of strangers,
interest in dance and song, and so forth. That such differences, sometimes

sharply marked, should occur between nearby communities has been long observed in Newfoundland (Wix quoted in Tucker, 1866:278). It is difficult to account for such variation when derivation, environment, economy, and cultural heritage are so similar.

The aim of this dissertation is the descriptive synthesis of a folk community from the point of view of the diagnostic aspect of its social structure and organization.

The first of these aspects (Chapter II) is the egalitarian nature of both the community and the "social area" in which the community exists. Both in Savage Cove and in the general area in which its inhabitants feel at ease we find an ethic of equality permeating social relationships. Differences in wealth and power are generally not great, and there is little specialization of labor. Equality is reflected in terms of address and in the general tone of relationships. This egalitarianism, and the comaradarie that accompanies it, facilitates relationships both within the community and with others in adjacent settlements.

The second (Chapter III) is the patrilocal extended family. This is the primary local social and economic unit. It comprises a fishing crew with all family members helping in catching or processing. As part of this system we find inheritance through men and a regular process of group segmentation. As residence is patrilocal, the settlements of the area are composed of a number of patrilines established by the original settlers: the names of the few early male residents have tended to remain the only ones in the community.

The extended family is the center of all the diverse activities engaged in by its members in making a living. Individual family members may go off to temporarily work for wages but these are contributed to the group. Also, various temporary contractural co-operating activities are engaged in between members of different family groups. The diverse techniques pursued in earning a living are described in Chapter IV. The fact that each man must do various things to make a living and the fact that what he does may vary according to expedience has prevented the development of any type of occupational identity.

Finally (in Chapter V) I have tried to typify the local mode of interpersonal relations. We find a pattern of withdrawal and permissiveness in social interaction in the area. This permits competitativeness between men in the area to exist without hampering intimate relations in a community in which there is a high degree of "role transparency."

These aspects of community life are related to a common historical and ecological situation. Newfoundland has always been an exporter of raw materials (either fish, wood, or minerals) and until around the turn of the century existed only as a producer of fish (plus some seal skins and furs). Very little soil is suitable for farming, there has been almost no manufacturing, and until around the turn of the century there was only one city, St. John's. There was little exchange on the island of food or other local products. Fish went out of the country and manufactured products came in. Also, government has always been remote from Newfoundland outports, particularly those on the west coast. For a long period of Newfoundland's history settlement was officially prohibited, and until 1904 the French had fishing rights on the west coast. At the present time there is (except for a community council in one settlement) no local government in the settlements along the Strait of Belle Isle.

The egalitarianism in the area is related, then, to a lack of formal organizational control and a lack of differentiation by wealth or occupation. Almost all men are primarily fishermen but work at various tasks and until recently barely managed to subsist. Perhaps it is not too gross a pun to say that egalitarianism is related to all being in the same boat.

Similarly, the diversity of labor on the part of each man is due to the marginal seasonal economic situation (one can only derive a limited return during a short period for any endeavor) with its lack of specialization and the necessity of producing most of what one needs. The extended family is the unit through which this labor is carried out. Having a large number of individuals working together is necessary in fishing and also insures an adequate number of people for the other important diverse tasks. It also enables men to go off, singly, and work in the lumber woods or other jobs for temporary periods while contributing incomes to the maintenance of the entire group.

The local mode of withdrawal and permissiveness in interpersonal relations is an adjustive mechanism in a competitive society and is related to a lack of formal political structure or status hierarchy. That is, allowing a wide range of permissible behavior is adaptive in an egalitarian society with little formal means of sanction because it reduces the probability of overt conflict.

One may also view the patrilocal extended family as the central institution in the area, a kin structure adapted to local fishing life. Given this, the mode of interaction and egalitarianism can be seen as ways of dealing with the non-formally structured social world outside the extended family.

The aspects of community life that I have selected are not only related to common antecedents but are inter-dependent. That they are diagnostic institutions possibly cannot be empirically demonstrated. However, others who have studied rural Newfoundland have indicated their presence. Chiaramonte (1966) discusses permissiveness and deviance in social relations as a key feature of life in a south coast Newfoundland fishing village. Co-operation between agnaticaly related nuclear families is an important feature of Cat Harbor, in the north-eastern part of the island (Faris, 1966) and is present, but not as frequently, in the Baie Verte area in the north central part of the island (Philbrook, 1966:62). In the latter area, however, even when close agnates do not make up crews . . .

> The structure of the work organization still
> followed familial lines; the relation between skipper
> and crewmen was like that between father and son, and
> between partners like that of brothers (Philbrook,
> 1966:72).

The competition and individuality which characterizes the Straits area seem to be present in the Baie Verte area. As one of Philbrook's (1966:70) informants states:

> When one man goes out sealing, all go. If one man
> gets five seals, all others try to beat him. But no
> man gets hurt by it; rather everyone benefits. . .
> When for example one man comes into the store and buys
> bullets then everyone knows he's going out sealing and
> they'll be there too. . . No one ever tells the other
> what he's doing. A man will come in and say "What d'ya
> doin' now, Earl?"--"Fixin' me trawl." This is all he
> says, no more! Every man is doing about the same thing
> but they don't talk about it, only with their partner.

ix

CHAPTER I

GEOGRAPHY, TOPONYMY, AND COMMUNITY

The island of Newfoundland forms a rough equilateral triangle with a
base along an east-west line and an apex pointing north. The two
features which most disturb the symmetry are the Avalon Peninsula,
containing the capital, St. John's, as well as half the population of
the island, appended at the southeast corner, and the indentations,
Notre Dame Bay and White Bay, on the northeast side. These leave the
northernmost part of the island a peninsula which juts up along the
west coast in a northeasterly direction.

At the end of this, the Great Northern Peninsula, lies the
Strait of Belle Isle, named after the steep-sided island in its northeast entrance, which separates the Island of Newfoundland from the
mainland. At its narrowest, from Flower's Cove on the Island to Point
Amour on the mainland, the Strait is nine miles across, and the coast
of Labrador is clearly visible from the Island on any good day. On
the other hand, it is a distance of about 93 miles across the Cabot
Strait from Port aux Basques, on the southwest tip, to North Sydney
on Cape Breton Island, Nova Scotia, a trip of six hours on the William
Carson, the Canadian National Railways ferry. The shortest distance
between the Island of Newfoundland and Cape Breton Island is about
sixty miles.

The triangle, Newfoundland, touches with its apex at the Strait
of Belle Isle, the southeast corner of Labrador. North of Belle Isle
the Labrador coast swings northward, but west of the Strait the coastline
forms the northern shore of the Gulf of St. Lawrence, and the southwest
corner of Newfoundland juts well into the Gulf. The southeastern corner
of the Island juts much further out in the Atlantic than the eastern
most point of Labrador, and Cape Spear, part of the same Avalon Peninsula
is the eastern most point in North America.

One may summarize the typography as follows:

> Essentially the island of Newfoundland consists
> of a tilted plateau of slight to moderate relief,
> rising northwestwards from the east coast. The
> western side of the island is almost mountainous,
> as the high plateau that rises to over 2,000 feet
> in some areas is heavily dissected. There are

Map I

Map of Newfoundland

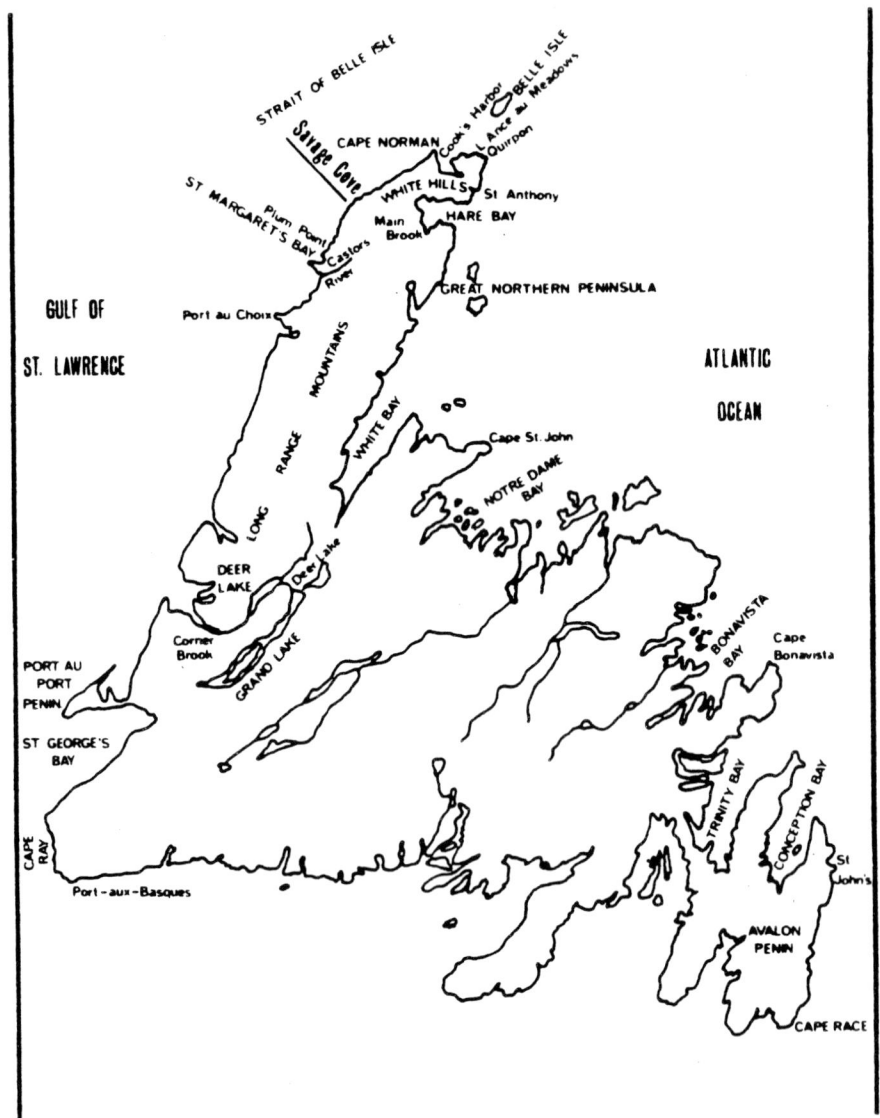

several deep, lake-studded basins that are almost
surrounded by hills, the Deer Lake and Grand Lake
basins being good examples. The central and
eastern parts of the plateau are lower and less
dissected, a large part of the island consisting
of a bleak, monotonously flat surface at 800 to
1500 feet. The easternmost region has been
extensively drowned, the old valleys now forming
large bays separated by elongated peninsulas
(Hare, 1952:36).

In general, northern and central portions of the main body of the
island, together with the Avalon Peninsula support "a good stand of close
forest," the primary types being white spruce and balsam fir. Across
the southern portion of the island, beginning at the Avalon Peninsula
and reaching to Cape Ray, stretch "moss barrens," great areas of "treeless
mossy and sedgy vegetation." These are also to be found on the Long
Range Mountains of the Great Northern Peninsula (1952:64-65).

Along the Long [Great Northern] Peninsula close
forest yields rapidly to open lichen woodland with
black spruce . . . growing scattered in a sea of
lichen . . . In the far north this in turn gives
way to a landscape in which tundra covers all but
the lowest ground--the so-called "forest tundra"
(1952:64).

The Labrador current is perhaps the major factor in the weather
of the island. This consists of cold water flowing south along the
Labrador coast. It strikes northern Newfoundland and bears along the
east coast, some of it rounding Cape Race and running along the south
coast, finally swinging north around Cape Ray to flow towards the Strait
of Belle Isle. This has the effect of cooling these areas in the summer,
but in the winter this water remains warmer than in other parts of the
Gulf of St. Lawrence "and the part of the gulf occupied by Labrador
current water is usually the least continuously frozen" (1952:38).

Sea ice also figures in Newfoundland's climate. Pack-ice drifts
down along the Labrador current and outward from the Gulf of St. Lawrence
on the Gaspe current, but some forms locally. The greatest extent of
sea-ice is in March, when typically it entirely surrounds the island
except for the south coast. This affects climate in that . . .

In summer, the presence of thawing ice-floes
keeps the sea temperature down to the freezing point.
The Labrador current bears great quantities of such
ice in May and June, and is hence able to retard the
spring rise of air temperature over the nearby coasts
(1952:39).

In winter these areas which are ice-free are considerably warmer than those that are ice-bound and a 20° F decrease in mean air temperature follows the packs' southward movement (1952:39). In January mean air temperatures approach 25 degrees on the south and east coasts, and are between 15 and 20 on the low elevations in the interior, and between 15 and 10 on the Northern Peninsula. Spring comes late as the pack-ice "keeps sea ice temperatures close to the freezing point until late May," and frosts are widespread in that month. July means vary from 50 to 60 degrees (41-5). On the whole then . . .

> . . . the presence of the sea reduces the observed
> extremes [in temperature] considerably, Newfoundland's
> reputation for bleak cold at all times is far from
> justified; in winter the whole island is milder, for
> example, than the Montreal plain, and in summer much
> of it compares well with Edmonton. The closest summer
> parallel is perhaps with southwest England (1952:41).

If the former quotation attempts to picture a milder climate for the island as a whole, the same article presents a more bleak picture for the Strait area.

> . . . the shores of Belle Isle Strait, at the
> northern end of the peninsula, have a near-Arctic
> climate in which forest patches can cling to the
> hillsides only in semi-prostrate form. This . . .
> results from the constant presence on both sides
> of the northern half of the peninsula of Labrador
> current water, often ice-laden well into July.
> Summer is hence a season of cool, drab weather,
> often accompanied by widespread fog or low stratus
> cloud. Belle Isle itself has a July mean temperature
> of only 49 degrees, in spite of its latitude (52
> degrees—that of London, England), and Cape Norman
> and St. Anthony on the mainland [of the Island of
> Newfoundland] are little warmer. No where else on
> earth does the Arctic drive so far south into
> middle latitudes (1952:47).

There has been a shift in population concentration away from Eastern Newfoundland which has gone along with the diminution of St. John's, the capital, as an economic center. Before the turn of the century fishing constituted the pre-eminent if not the sole means of Newfoundland's support. Not until the turn of the century was the position of St. John's, at the eastern extremity of the island, influenced by western development. The railway linking the eastern and western shores of the island was built and the treaty rights the

French had had to fish on the West Coast ended. Not long after an
extensive pulp wood industry was established in the west and central
parts of the island and mineral developments commenced on a large
scale. Along with this the output of the central and western fisheries
increased (Copes, 1961:18).

> The gradual shift westward of the economic centre
> of gravity in Newfoundland is reflected in census
> population statistics which have been collected since
> 1836 . . . . At that time almost 95 percent of the
> Island's population were resident in the eastern
> extremities--Burin, Avalon, and Bonavista. At the
> turn of the century, Eastern Newfoundland accounted
> for little more than 70 percent of the total, and
> today for about 56 percent only. The Avalon
> Peninsula, where the major share of Eastern Newfound-
> land's population is concentrated, was reduced from
> 73 percent of the Island's total in 1836 to 41 percent
> in 1956.

> While Eastern Newfoundland's relative importance
> has diminished, the area's population has continued
> to expand in absolute terms. In fact, during the
> period 1836-1956, the population more than trebled,
> reaching a total of 233,402 in the latter year.
> However, central and western portions of the Island
> (not including Labrador), over the same period,
> experienced a phenomenal 43-fold increase in population
> --from 4,000 to almost 174,000. Newfoundland as a
> whole registered a five- to six-fold increase, reaching
> a recorded population total of 415,074 in 1956 (1956:21).

Prior to these developments the only settlement was along the
coast, so until around the turn of the century the interior of the
country was almost completely uninhabited. Tiny fishing settlements
ringed the coastline with St. John's the only city. Such interior
towns as Gander, Grand Falls and Deer Lake are a recent development.

The largest urban population concentration is the St. John's
Metropolitan Area with 77,991 in 1956. It is predicted that it will
reach 150,000 by 1980 (1961:21). The next largest community is
Corner Brook on the West Coast with a population of 25,185 in 1961.
Also on the West Coast, Stephenville, at Harmon Field, a United States
Air Force base, had a population of 6,043 the same year and the adjacent
Stephenville Crossing, 2,209. Deer Lake, at the bottom of the Great
Northern Peninsula had 3,998. The largest population on the Great
Northern Peninsula are at St. Anthony which has somewhat over 2,000
and Roddickton with 1,185 (Census of Canada, 1961). The more than 1200

settlements which line Newfoundland's more than 6000 miles of coastline
are very small in size, those along the Strait of Belle Isle, at least,
running all under 350.

Savage Cove, the fishing settlement that is the subject of this
study, is situated on the Strait of Belle Isle near the tip of the
Great Northern Peninsula which, some 40 miles wide, extends some 140
miles northward from the western side of the island. The road that
links the Newfoundland shore of the Strait to the rest of the Island
to the south has been open only since November 1962. A road leading to
St. Anthony to the northeast, the largest settlement on the Peninsula,
has been open a few years longer.

Prior to this, transportation was only by coastal steamer and
small boat in the summer, dog team, and more recently, horse drawn
sled and snowmobile, in the winter. The "coastal boats," small
steamers, carry freight and passengers to the various settlements, and
before the government wharfs were put in about nine years ago they
anchored in the coves, and goods and passengers were loaded and unloaded
by small boats. Due to the winter ice, the settlements were isolated
from January to June before the road came through, and merchants had
to stock up before the last coastal boat came through in December.
Sometimes in the spring, if supplies were running low, the government
would try to get an early ship through the late ice.

The new road runs up the western shore of the Peninsula, along
a flat coastal strip from which the Long Range Mountains can be seen
in the distance running parallel to the coast. These present a steep
bunlike face as they rise up to around 2000 feet from the level land.
This highland goes right to the sea on the opposite side of the Peninsula,
and there the coast is marked by precipitous cliffs sheltering tiny
settlements in deeply cut inlets.

Northward on the east coast the hills run out in the vicinity of
Plum Point some 50 miles from Cape Norman, the northwest tip of the
Peninsula. Except for the White Hills in the St. Anthony area, this
northernmost portion is flat marshy land broken by patches of woods
and innumerable ponds. This area, from the end of the Long Range
Mountains to Cape Norman and east across the country to Hare Bay,
forms the hinterland of the settlements along the Newfoundland shore

of the southwest half of the Strait. All habitation is along the coast, but men go into the interior for wood and to hunt.

Each settlement has its wood path going "into the country." These paths are oriented so as to cross as many ponds as possible, and wood is not hauled out until they are frozen over, thus providing much easier going for sleds over the snow-covered, level pond ice. This practice is depicted in the Newfoundland song "Tickle Cove Pond" which commemorates the immersion of a wood-hauler and his mare after the former ignored the unspoken advice of the latter regarding the fragility of the late spring ice. It begins:

> In cuttin' and haulin' in frost and in snow,
> We're up against troubles that few people know,
> And only patience, with courage and grit,
> And eatin' plain food, can we keep ourselves fit.
> The hard and the aisey we take as it comes,
> And when ponds freeze over we shorten our runs.
> (Mills and Peacock, 1958:8-9).

When travelling the wood paths on foot when the ice is gone you skirt the shorelines of the ponds ("land-washes'n") to return to where the path goes overland between the little lakes. Along the paths one encounters a series of ponds, meshes [marshes], wood covered rudges [ridges], and nudiks [small groves of trees]. Going into the country along the Savage Cove path one traverses Meadow Pond, Little Pinch Pond, Big Pinch Pond, The Pinch (rudge), Big Pond, Big Pond Rudge, Dempster's Pond, Dempster's Rudge, a lade [glade], Hay Pond, Hay Pond Rudge, L'Anch (rudge), the Lake, Beaver House Pond, Browse Pond, Harry Way's Rudge, and so on.

The smaller ponds and flashets [tiny ponds] are often found in the middle of marshes, while the larger ones are usually surrounded by woods. As the land is flat and marshy, there is often no obvious drainage between the smaller ponds, but the larger are connected by small brooks and steadies[1] whose flow meanders and eventually empties into the sea by way of the larger brooks. All the major interior geographical features are locally named, but few of these names appear on maps. People state that it is necessary that they be named so that one can explicitly designate a location, and this is probably also important as there are no outstanding physical features to guide one in the interior. One is told that "the old people were pretty smart to have put names on everything."

The Newfoundland settlements along the Straits of Belle Isle
cluster towards its entrances: at the southwest from Anchor Point[2] to
Eddies Cove,[3] and at the northeast from Boat Harbour, about five miles
southwest of Cape Norman, to Quirpon.[4] This leaves a central gap
between Eddies Cove and Boat Harbour which is broken only by Big Brook,
about ten miles southwest of Boat Harbour. There was also at one time
a settlement of Four Mile Cove, four miles southwest of Big Brook.
This gap is explained by the straight exposed coast which constitutes
the shoreline in this area, and is marked as "Straight Coast" on some
of the early maps[5] (Seary, 1960:135).

From Anchor Point to Cape Norman the coastline consists largely
of rock shelves, and when the wind and tide drive the waves shoreward
they smash against these shelves sending spray high into the air. At
low tide they can be seen exposed looking much like huge steps leading
downward under the water, but in some places the rock has been smashed
into boulders by the waves.

This rock lies very close under the soil in an unbroken mass.
The entire area is "all one junk" [chunk], as one resident put it.
It is difficult to dig a deep well without drilling equipment, and in
some places it is hard to dig a sufficiently deep grave. The flat
surface of the rock sheet can be seen at the bottom of shallow coastal
ponds where it appears exposed like a solid core as if the thin skin
of soil had been peeled away.

In contrast with the lowland on much of the Newfoundland side,
the Labrador shore rises steeply and is pierced by deep bays: Forteau
Bay, L'Anse au Loup, and Pinware Bay. The dramatically steep cliffs
between the first two inlets are known as "The Battery," and are quite
impressive from the Newfoundland shore. From Savage Cove one can look
directly across the Strait to the lighthouse at Point Amour. As this
is the narrowest part of the Strait, some nine miles across, it can be
seen clearly on a good day, and at night one can see its light as well
as the light on Greenly Island,[6] some 25 miles west and about five
miles south of the Labrador Coast. This island and Ile au Bois, just
east of it, are sometimes faintly visible as a low line on the horizon
from Savage Cove. Just to the right of these can be seen, on any clear
day, the headland which marks the most westerly part of the Labrador
visible from Savage Cove. From Savage Cove it appears as an island

Map II

Map of the Strait of Belle Isle

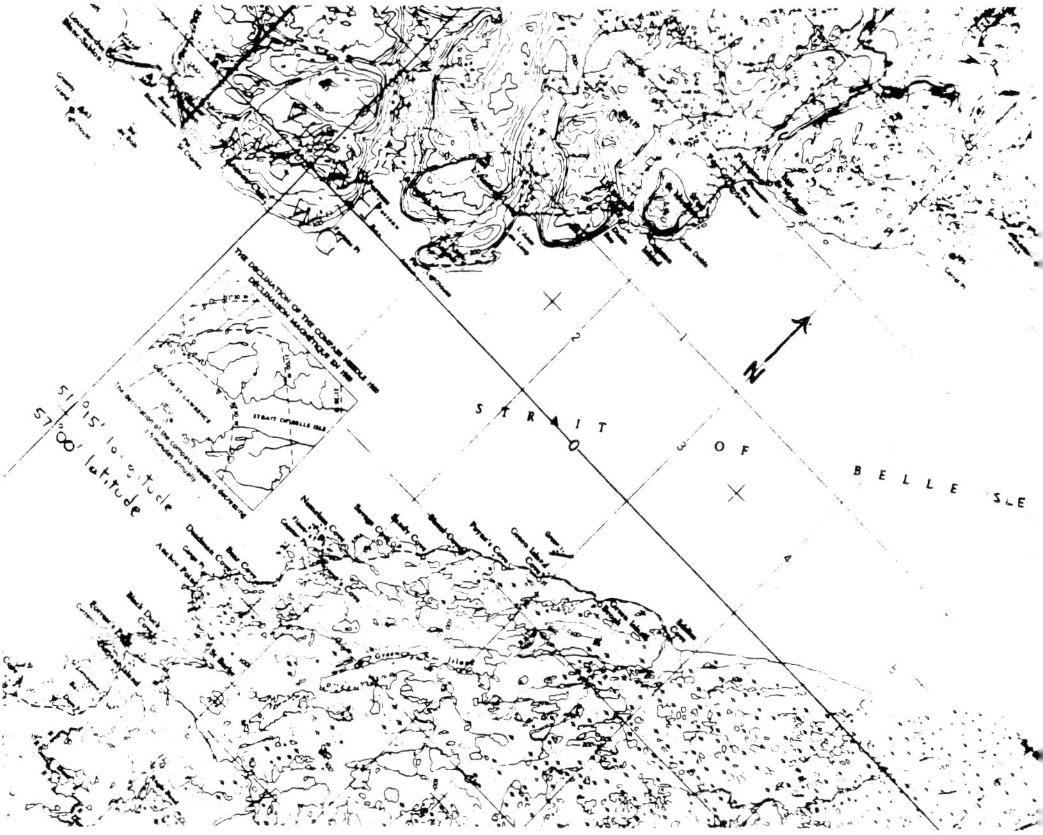

since the valley of the Riviere Blanc-Sablon which separates it from the highland to the east lies below the horizon. The evening sun sometimes produces a mirage in which the headland appears to float slightly above the horizon.

The land on the Labrador side of the Strait is a desolate "coastal tundra" which rises in folds to the woodlands far in the interior. This barren ground is a general feature of the south-east Labrador coast.

> This sterile coastal area is evident, most continuous and most shocking to the eye, from just west of Cape Whittle to just beyond Battle Harbour. The north shore of the Strait of Belle Isle belongs to this belt; its grim rocky aspect has been immortalized by Cartier's famous obloquy.

> "J'estime, mieulx que sultrement, que c'est la tere que Dieu donna a Cayn," which he uttered after inspecting the coast near Blanc Sablon (Hare and Taylor, 1956:63).

The Strait is on a main shipping lane between the St. Lawrence and Europe, and on summer nights the lights of the steamers can be seen strung out in line far into the distance.

> The Island lies athwart the great circle route from the middle and northern Atlantic ports of North America to Western and Northern Europe, and ships following this route must detour north through the Strait of Belle Isle or south of Cape Race. The northern route, however, is used almost entirely by ships from St. Lawrence River ports and is open and safe for navigation only during late summer and early autumn months. Even on the southern route the shipping lanes shift southward in certain seasons and in certain years due to hazards of fog and ice (MacKay, 1946:41).

There is some directional terminology in the Strait which may confuse the stranger. First of all, down designates a northernly direction, and up designates a southernly direction. This obtains throughout Newfoundland. Locally the Strait is thought to run east and west, whereas, west of Cape Norman, they actually run northeast to southwest, and similarly, it is felt that directly across the Strait is north rather than northwest. This is because magnetic north is about northwest in the Strait, the declination is around $31^\circ00'$ W, and people go by their compass readings.[7] Consequently, they speak of going

11

eastern [in the direction of Cape Norman] and going western [in the
direction of Corner Brook]. Here I shall use up and down as indicating
north and south respectively and mean true, rather than magnetic north
and other directions, respectively.

Savage Cove lies not too far from a point halfway between Anchor
Point at the southwest entrance to the Strait (James, 1937:51) and
Eddies Cove. Anchor Point is the oldest settlement in the area having
been founded around 1740. It was also a center of dispersal for the
early settlers in the area as many worked for the Genge family at
Anchor Point before moving on to settle in the other coves (Richards,
1953a:18, 1953b:15).

Flower's Cove[8] is the political and economic center of the area.
It contains the Canon Richards Memorial High School which serves the
Flower's Cove Mission (Anglican) and is the only one in the area,
attracting pupils from outside the mission and, until recently, from
the adjacent Labrador. It also has the Anglican parsonage and St.
Barnabas Church, the major one in the mission. The regional welfare
officer lives in Flower's Cove, as does the regional fisheries officer.
There are two garages, a large modern restaurant where one can get full
meals, a barber shop, and two snack bars, amusement parlor "restaurants."
There is also a small hotel, a boarding house, the Canadian National
Railways telegraph office, the head post office for the area, and the
regional (St. Barbe's) cooperative. There are at least three merchants
in Flower's Cove who carry a large variety of goods, in contrast to some
of the small shops in most of the other settlements.

Until World War I the only merchants in the Straits were in
Flower's Cove. This meant that people had to walk long distances to
get their supplies when there was no snow on the ground and to travel
to Flower's Cove by dog team during winter. Boats could be used in the
summer, but there was much walking, and those who do not own cars and
trucks still do a great deal of walking between the communities. Although
there are merchants with large stocks in Savage Cove and in Sandy Cove,
it is still necessary to go to Flower's Cove to make purchases of one
kind or another.

The Grenfell Nursing Station is also at Flower's Cove. Here a
daily clinic and small hospital are maintained by the two nurses in

residence, and a physician from the Grenfell hospital in St. Anthony holds a clinic every two weeks when possible. There is also a public health nurse who visits from Eddies Cove East to south of Port Saunders.

From Deadman's Cove (the settlement northeast of Anchor Point) to Eddies Cove the settlements in the Strait have the same names as the coves in which they stand. The only exception to this is Green Island Brook, between Green Island Cove and Eddies Cove. So, from southwest to northeast, we have Deadman's Cove, Flower's Cove, Nameless Cove, Mistaken Cove (not a settlement), Savage Cove, Sandy Cove, Shoal Cove, Payne's Cove,[9] Green Island Cove, and Eddies Cove. Green Island Brook is named after the stream which empties into the Strait at that point. The same is true of Big Brook, further up the coast.

In order to differentiate between the coves and the names of settlements when they are the same I shall underline the names of Coves when referring specifically to them.

There are a number of local place names in the area which differ from the names on the maps.[10] For instance, what is on the map as Flower's Cove (cove and settlement) is locally called French Island Harbour, and what is on the map as Nameless Cove (cove and settlement) is called Flower's Cove. According to Canon Richards the name French Island Harbour is based upon the old name for the island that lies to the south of the entrance to the cove which was called French Island after the French who used it in their summer fishing operations.

> James Chambers . . . settled in Bear Cove, three miles west of Flower's Cove. In summer he moved out to Seal Island, which was also called French Island, because it had been a favorite resort of the French fishermen. What is now called Flower's Cove, was first called French Island Harbour. The island was a lovely spot in summer, and was separated from the low flat mainland by a tickle not more than twenty five yards wide. Through this tickle every spring, great numbers of old harps and bedlamers passed on their migration eastward through the Strait of Belle Isle (1953b:15).

On the National Topographic Series map of the area this island and the smaller islands around it are collectively called Seal Islands, and on the land grant map it is called Fish Island. It is referred to locally now as Chamber's Island, the tickle[11] as Chamber's tickle, and a small island in the tickle is called the Pancake. The small islet southwest of it is referred to locally as Duck Island, and the islet to the west of it as Scotland. However, Canon Richards seemed to consider French Island to be Scotland:

> In the summer of 1853 . . . a Scotch vessel named the "Orkney" ran on the island [italics mine] of French Island Cove. This island is now called Scotland. After throwing a lot of her cargo away, she got off again (Richards, 1953b:23).

The large pond inland from Flower's Cove is French Island Pond, both on the maps and locally.

The settlement of Flower's Cove occupies both sides of Flower's Cove, the thickest settlement being on the north shore. The settlement of Nameless Cove occupies the north shore of that cove, the next one north. In Nameless Cove are to be found Herb Island, locally called Green Island, and Flower's Island, locally called Joey's Island, after Joe Levelle, the now deceased keeper of the lighthouse which stands upon it.

The next cove northeast is Mistaken Cove on the maps but is locally known as Shoal Cove, to be specific, Middle Shoal Cove as there are two others, Shoal Cove West and Shoal Cove East. There are few houses on its southwest shore, which are considered "Shoal Cove houses," but whether or not it is a separate settlement from Nameless Cove is moot.

Savage Cove is some nine-tenths of a mile northeast of Mistaken Cove. The little peninsula that separates them is wide as compared to the narrow strips on which Nameless Cove and Flower's Cove are built. This land consists of a low hill rising gently on the Mistaken Cove side, but having a sharper escarpment on the Savage Cove side. Its sides are parallel for half its length, but converge to form Yankee Point at its tip. It is ringed with small trees and at its center is Bakeapple Pond and Bakeapple Mesh, on which many of the bakeapples consumed by the people of Savage Cove are gathered. This fruit is considered the most delicious of all the wild berries available.

The highroad,[12] largely following the old path between communities, proceeds from Flower's Cove, passes the Nameless Cove branch and dips down into a small valley at the bottom of Mistaken Cove (Shoal Cove). Here it crosses Shoal Cove Brook, a fine place to "get a meal of whitefish" [smelt] in the spring when they swim up some of the small brooks to the

Map III

Savage Cove

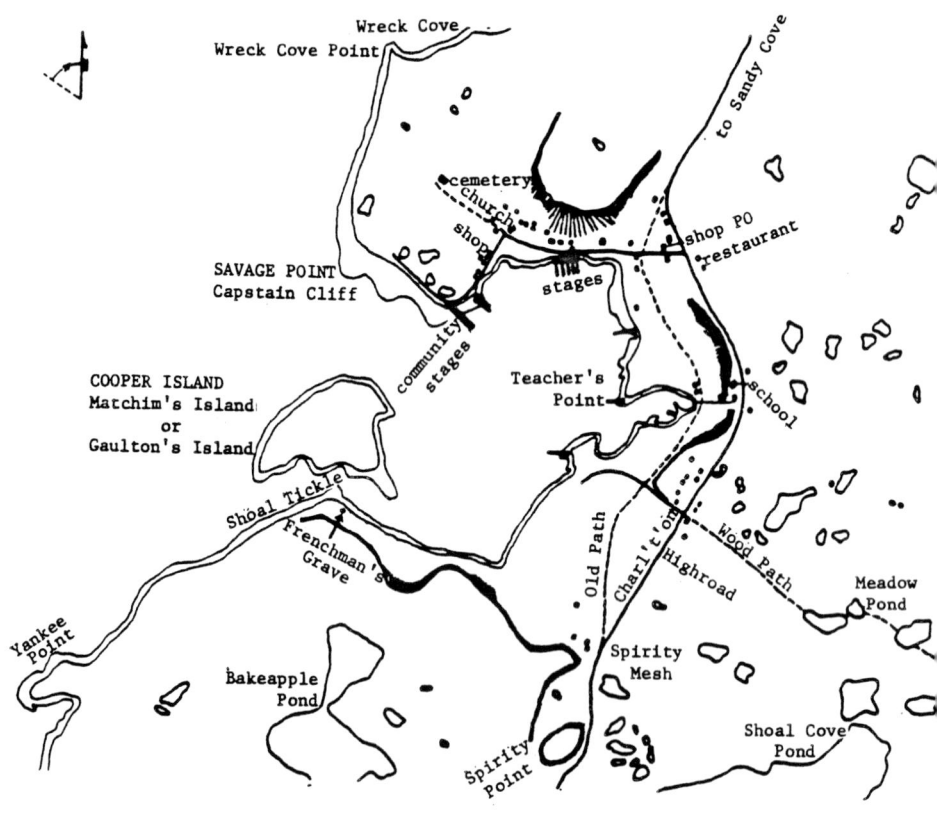

ponds from which they flow. The road then rises up Shoal Cove Hill and
rounds Spirity Point, part of the southeastern slope of the rise on the
peninsula between Mistaken Cove and Savage Cove. It then crosses Spirity
Mesh named, as the point, for a headless figure once seen walking there.
Going northeast across the mesh, the edge of the escarpment turns to the
northwest to form the southwest (left) side of Savage Cove. Once past
the mesh the road crosses the high meadow from which one can see all of
Savage Cove.

Savage Cove contains a small island, which according to the
topographic map is Cooper Island, at the southwestern side of its mouth.
It is known locally as Gaulton's Island by the older residents of Savage
Cove, as the Gaulton's lived there first, and as Matchim's (pronounced
Maxim) Island by the younger, as Matchim's lived there later. It is
separated from the mainland by a narrow tickle, Shoal Tickle, which is
dry at low tide. Sandy Cove cows walk along the highroad to Savage Cove
and sometimes wander across the tickle at low tide to graze on the island.

At low tide the southwest side of the cove has a fairly straight
and pebbly beach running all the way to Cooper Island. Clams abound in
these sands but are not eaten locally. Behind this beach runs the
wooded ridge which is the northeast side of the peninsula separating
Mistaken Cove and Savage Cove.

In shape Savage Cove resembles a narrow necked flask. The left
side is formed by the straight southwest shore. The constricted neck
is formed on the left side by Cooper Island jutting out into the cove
and on the right by a neck of land which extends out between the northeast side of the cove and the sea. This neck ends in Savage Point,
called Capstan Cliff locally because the capstan of the seal frame used
to be placed there in the spring. The main part of the settlement of
Savage Cove lies along the right hand side of the cove and along the
right hand side of the bottom of the cove. Here a small inlet divides
the community separating Savage Cove proper from that section which lies
along the left hand side of the bottom of the cove and is known locally
as Charl't'on.

As the highroad descends from a meadow it parallels the bottom of
the cove. Charl't'on has its own little branch near the lower left hand
corner of the cove, and the branch for the main part of the settlement

is on the right hand side of the cove. The highroad runs along a rise at the bottom of the cove, and this high ground continues on the right side of the cove up to the neck of land which ends in Savage Point.

About half a mile up from Savage Point is a point called Wreck Cove Point, which marks the western end of Wreck Cove; both are local names.

The houses in the main part of the settlement are generally oriented in an irregular line facing the cove, although recently some have been built back along the highroad. This line runs parallel to the branch which follows the shoreline. Along the north side of the cove the houses are built along the hillside that also follows the shoreline. Behind the houses are cleared meadows which were once kept for hay but now serve for general grazing. Near the end of the hill the branch makes an abrupt left turn to follow the shoreline as it bends inwards towards the cove and at this point is located the settlement's small church. Along the road beyond the turn is the shop of one of the merchants. The other merchant is to be found near the point where the branch leaves the highroad, and the post office is located in his shop. The school is located along the bottom of the cove at the lower end of the main part of the settlement so as to make it near Charl't'on.

Charl't'on is composed of a group of houses on either side of the highroad at the bottom of the meadow. It is composed of families that have moved into the settlement in recent years and of families that lived scattered out around the south side of the cove. Some of the latter's old houses and stables remain on the top of the meadows above spirity Point.

The population of the settlements in the area vary downward from that of Flower's Cove which has 312 individuals. The following were the populations in 1961: Anchor Point, 223; Bear Cove, 169; Nameless Cove, 61; Savage Cove, 234; Sandy Cove, 202; Payne's Cove, 79; Green Island Cove, 174; Green Island Brook, 190; and Eddies Cove, 149. There were no figures for Deadman's Cove, Mistaken Cove, Shoal Cove East, Lower Cove, and Big Brook in the 1961 Canadian Census, but this is undoubtedly because communities with populations of less than fifty are not listed (Census of Canada, 1961). They were all cited with populations of less than fifty in the 1935 Newfoundland census (Census of Newfoundland, 1935).

CHAPTER II

THE SOCIAL AREA AND ITS HISTORY

Any small community exists in a field composed of other communities and, in more complex societies, individuals representing urban life. This is true for a hunting and gathering people like the Siriono who rarely even encounter bands of fellow tribesmen, and it is true for Yucatan villages who maintain relations with adjacent communities and a central government (Redfield, 1955:113-131).

There are always relationships with the outside and these have a certain nature and extend over a certain distance. Such relationships may be of an ethnic, economic, political or religious nature. There will be some sort of boundary, or boundaries, which separates those who are meaningfully connected to the communities from those who are not, or who are less so related. There is a limitation or a series of limitations to the social world.

Another dimension to this type of relationship is that of how any community perceives those who are around it. What types of people populate their conceptual as well as their spacial universe?

In order to explore these factors for Savage Cove I shall discuss the area which includes the settlements closest to it under the rubric of the "social area." What I wish to stress most about the social area and Savage Cove itself is the egalitarian attitude that characterizes them. Conceptions of peoples outside the area will be taken up, but first it is necessary to briefly trace the history of Newfoundland and the Strait of Belle Isle in order to follow the development of the social area.

A Short History of Newfoundland

The history of European settlement in Newfoundland must now be recorded from approximately 1000 A.D. when a group of Norsemen wintered in L'anse au Meadows, a cove on the northern tip of the Great Northern Peninsula. Dr. Helmut Ingstad has found abundant evidence that it was in fact a Norse settlement and carbon-14 dating has placed the time. The site consists of several buildings including a miltiroomed structure typical of Norse settlements at that time and, most important, a smithy where ore was worked (Ingstad, 1964).

European contact appears to have been broken from that point until
June 24, 1497 when John Cabot made a landfall the exact location of which
is unknown. Labrador, Newfoundland, and Cape Breton all claim the honor.
It is possible, however, that French and Spanish boats had been fishing
on the Grand Banks for some years before the English arrived.[1] The
English were not long in following Cabot; as early as 1503 Newfoundland
is mentioned in English records.

At first the English were content to trade with the French or to
capture their cargoes of fish, and the Portuguese did much of the
exploring giving to Newfoundland many Portuguese place names; but by
1560 the West Country fishery was on its way to being economically
important and was further encouraged when restrictions were imposed on
English ships fishing off Iceland.

It was not until the 1580's that England began to view Newfoundland and her fishery as important to her national power, and then began
an effort to oust the Spanish which lasted some thirty years. At this
time Newfoundland was still a zone of international competition and
England had not yet pressed a claim based on Cabot's discovery. Then in
1583 Sir Humphrey Gilbert, half-brother to Sir Walter Raleigh, arrived
in St. John's and took possession of St. John's harbour and all the land
for 200 leagues in all directions for the Queen and his heirs; however,
this had little immediate effect and Gilbert was lost at sea on his
homeward voyage.

There was no official colonization as yet, but the English method
of curing fish required shore space and facilities. Allotment of shore
space was strictly a first-come-first-choice affair, and the facilities
of one year seldom survived to be used the next. What law there was
supplied by the "fishing admiral" who held his position by virtue of
being the first captain in port. An attempt at more permanent structures
necessitated leaving a member of the crew to look after the buildings
during the winter, although this was discouraged by the English government.

During the 17th century when the importance of sea power became
evident, interest in the Newfoundland fishery shifted from the
consideration of commercial profit to the need for trained seamen, and
the Newfoundland fishery came to be seen as a "nursery for seamen." The

first official plantations were established at this time and were
harrassed by the French and Dutch, as well as by English West Country
fishermen who complained that the colonists took the best fishing berths
and in other ways hindered them. As a result the colonists were
constrained from cutting wood or building within six miles of the coast.

The Treaty of Utrecht in 1713 was important for Newfoundland.
Although England gained sovereign right to the island, the French were
given the right to fish and to make [process] their fish on the north
and west coasts between Bonavista and Cape Riche. As far as settlement
was concerned the British policy continued to be based on the conviction
that a fishery carried on from England would be beneficial to British
sea power, and consequently settlement was discouraged. Despite
restrictions to the contrary immigration to Newfoundland continued and
the population increased.

By the end of the first decade of the 19th century Newfoundland
had progressed to the point where it was no longer possible to ignore
its settlement, and in 1815 a full time governor was appointed to
replace the yearly fishing admiral. The Napoleonic wars helped to
implement the change from fishing station to settlement colony by
virtually ending both the British and French annual voyages to the island.
The fishing was left to the colonists who had several things in their
favor: improved shipping, growth of the sealing industry which provided
employment during the off season, and the fact that the making of fish
lent itself to the use of family labor which was much cheaper than outside labor.

In 1817 for the first time the Governor was instructed to winter
in Newfoundland. A council to assist the Governor was appointed for
the first time in 1825, and in 1832 representative assembly was granted
the Colony. For the next few years, there was, unfortunately, a good
deal of dissension and some violence. Finally in 1855, after much
conflict, Newfoundland was granted full responsible government.

With the end of the Napoleonic wars the French resumed fishing
on the Grand Banks and the French shore and became serious competitors
to the local fishery. After much discussion and negotiation over the
French fishing rights and the Treaty Shore the Pigeard-Mericale
Convention was signed in London on January 14, 1857. This agreement

provided that the French would have exclusive fishing rights on the west coast from Cape St. John to the Quirpon Islands and on the north coast from the Quirpon Islands to Cape Norman and were granted five specified harbors on the west coast; Newfoundlanders were allowed to fish with the French from Cape Norman to Cape Ray except at the five harbours; the French could fish on the Labrador with the Newfoundlanders; the French gained the right to buy bait on the south coast and, under certain conditions, to fish for bait; the French navy was empowered to enforce the fishing rights; and the Newfoundlanders were not to build on the strand set aside exclusively for the French. This treaty was naturally unpopular in Newfoundland. In the face of the colony's opposition to the treaty the British government admitted that, since it had not been ratified by the Newfoundland legislature, it was null and void. Then followed almost fifty years of negotiation and renegotiation; the question of the Newfoundland French Shore was not settled until the Anglo-French Convention of 1904 when France gave up her rights in Newfoundland in return for concessions elsewhere.

During the 18th century the United States was also involved in treaty negotiations over fishing rights in Newfoundland waters, but feelings about the U.S. fishery were not as strong as those about the French, and the U.S. trade declined gradually after the middle of the century.

In 1864 a conference was held in Charlottetown, Prince Edward Island, on the question of the confederation of the Atlantic colonies with Canada. Although Newfoundland had no representative at this conference she did send two representatives to the Quebec meeting held in October of that year. At first the outlook for confederation was good in Newfoundland, but before it could be achieved public opinion changed, and this coupled with problems over the French Shore kept Newfoundland out of the Canadian confederation.

At the beginning of the First World War the Newfoundland economy seemed strong, the French Shore problems were over, and exploitation of the natural resources, other than the fishery, was beginning. During the war the Royal Newfoundland Regiment distinguished itself at the Battle of the Somme. The 1920 deflation hit Newfoundland hard as the economic boom of the war years had been built on credit. This depression which was the worst in Newfoundland history spelled the end of self-government. In 1933 the Amulree Commission met in St. John's to consider Newfoundland's political and economic situation and make recommendations to the British government. They recommended a commission form of government for the island with the United Kingdom assuming responsibility for the finances of Newfoundland until such time as the island again became self-supporting. The commission of six men, three Englishmen and three Newfoundlanders, was established in 1934 and continued until 1947. The credit for Newfoundland's return to relative prosperity belongs not to the Commission Government, but to the conditions brought about by World War II. Newfoundland occupied a strategic position in the defense of the North Atlantic, and consequently both the United States and Canada built and maintained air bases on the island, pouring money into the island's economy.

By the end of the war the people of Newfoundland were anxious to be free of the Commission rule, and Britain was not anxious to continue to be responsible for Newfoundland. In 1946 a Convention met to consider the political and economic future of Newfoundland. One of the leaders at the Convention was Joseph R. Smallwood, an ardent pro-Confederationist. It was due largely to his efforts that Newfoundland joined the Canadian Confederation. Smallwood was invited to form a government until a provincial election could be held and has been Premier since.

Confederation with Canada has meant a great deal to Newfoundland: pensions, baby bonuses, family allowances. The people of Newfoundland are enjoying a better standard of living than would have been believed possible fifty years ago. The price for fish is increasing, the lumber industry is growing, there are two or three mines operating on the island, and the government is exploring the possibilities of other mineral resources and oil. There are plans for utilizing the as-yet-unharnessed potential hydro-power of the Labrador rivers. The island's fish and game have already attracted many sportsmen, and the provincial government is now working to promote the tourist industry by capitalizing on the natural beauty of the island (MacKay, 1946, Perlin, 1959). Regarding the derivation of the population:

> Most Newfoundlanders are native born and
> ethnically homogeneous. In 1961 slightly over
> 96 per cent of the population was native to the

Province. Two-thirds of the Newfoundlanders came
from the English West Country, mainly from Somerset,
Dorset, and Devon; about a fourth came from Ireland
and the Channel Islands. In the Codroy Valley--on
the island's southwest coast--there are a number of
farming settlements composed of French Acadians who
migrated from Nova Scotia in the first half of the
eighteenth century.

In Newfoundland there is a sprinkling of Micmac
Indians who came to the island from Nova Scotia in
the eighteenth century. After being reduced in
numbers by continuous wars with the Micmacs, the
original Indian population--the Beothics--were wiped
out by the English in the nineteenth century. Also
in the region of St. George Bay, there are settlements
of Jackatars of a French and Indian mixture (Philbrook,
1966:13-14).

A History of Settlement in the Strait of Belle Isle

According to Canon J. T. Richards (1953a:17), an Anglican
priest who spent some forty years in the Strait of Belle Isle, the
first settlement on the French Shore was at Anchor Point. The French
Shore, or the Treaty Shore, was the coastal strip from Cape Ray to Cape
St. John along which, until 1904, the French had the right to catch and
make fish during the summer. They could not, however, build fortifica-
tions, or permanent structures, or remain on the coast after their fish
were dried. The French Shore ran some 535 miles from the southwest tip
of Newfoundland and along the western shore, around the tip of the Great
Northern Peninsula, down its eastern side, around the shores of White
Bay, and over to Cape St. John on the western end of Notre Dame Bay
(Togue, 1878:234). Settlement along this shore was forbidden, though
people gradually trickled into the area.

Canon Richards approximates the arrival of the first settler, Robert
Bartlett, at Anchor Point as not later than 1750. The story of the
arrival was told to Richards by Thomas Genge--Bartlett was his father's
great uncle--who gave the date as 1740.

It seems that Bartlett and a companion had gone ashore to get wood
from a boat in White Bay. While on shore they were captured by "Red
Indians" who forced them to carry their burdens. That night the pair,
as they were not tied when the group went to sleep around a large fire,
made their escape. They travelled overland across the Great Northern
Peninsula until they came to the western side at what is now Anchor Point,

and there they saw an American schooner whose crew was making their fish.
Bartlett decided to settle there and persuaded the American captain to
fit him out. He sent word with his companion, who left with the schooner
on his way back to England, to his nephew Robert Genge in Yeovil,
Somerset, asking him to come out and picturing the area as abounding in
cod, seals, game, and wild fruits.

Robert Genge came the next year, and the two lived alone for a
number of years until Bartlett sent to Yeovil for another nephew, Abram
Genge. The latter became the leader[2] of the group and as Englishmen and
Scots arrived in the area he hired them and assigned each a certain
section of the coast to hunt and fish. He became quite wealthy, and the
fish and furs he gathered in were taken away by American schooners.
After working for Genge for a time the newcomers would settle down on
their own on some section of the coast.

Up to this point there were no women on the coast, but these were
to be supplied by the Watts family. Watts was employed by Abram Genge
on a part of the shore near Boat Harbour, and had two sons and two
daughters. William Buckle and his son, William, arrived about this
time and went to work for Abram Genge in St. Margaret's Bay. After the
elder Buckle died, the younger trapped for a time on Belle Isle, then
lived at Lanse au Clair with Peter St. Clair, after whom that settlement
was named. After this he became the first permanent settler of Forteau
but then moved back to Anchor Point where he married one of Watts'
daughters. Buckle fished at Forteau during the summer but, after his
boys grew up, lived at Buckle's Point in St. Margaret's Bay during the
winter. From this marriage are descended all the Buckles living on the
Labrador today.

About the time Watts' daughter was married to Buckle, somewhere
between 1795 and 1800, a naval lieutenant named Alexander Duncan
deserted from the British warship patrolling the coast to marry her
sister. Duncan went to work for Genge and assumed his mother's maiden
name, Gould, to avoid detection. Alexander Duncan and Mary Watts had
"three sons, and no less than fourteen children, who grew into beautiful
girls" [sic] (Richards, 1953a:19). The latter supplied wives for the
Englishmen and Scots who were then coming into the area.

Philip Coates, the first settler of Eddies Cove East, married their daughter Sarah. Thomas Mitchelmore, the first settler of Green Island Cove, took another as his first wife. George Coles[3] and Thomas White,[4] first permanent settlers of Sandy Cove,[5] married Ann[4] and Eliza Duncan.[4] Susan[4] married George Gaulton, the first settler of Savage Cove. William Coombs and William Dredge were the first settlers of Black Duck Cove, and they married two of the daughters, Dredge's wife being Margaret.[4]

Again a Genge was sent for from Yeovil when Abram Genge, as an old man, sent for his nephew William. William married one of William Buckle's daughters, and all the Genges in the Strait are descended from him. James Chambers, an early settler of Bear Cove, married Jane, another of Buckle's daughters.

Prior to 1851 most of the settlers were English and Scots, and how they happened to come to the area is not, for the most part, recorded. However, one William Griffin, a huge Scot[6] who was called Big William, was employed by the North West Company in Labrador, and came to be employed by Genge to fish Castor River after leaving his old job grief stricken after killing another Scot in a fight. He was an excellent fiddler, was beloved by the children, and had a head so large that no hat could be found to fit it. A hat was obtained for him only after the captain of an English warship took the measurement of his head and had a hat made to order in England. Once a boat that was being launched slipped off the ways and stuck in the mud. Four men could not budge her, but Big William, ill at the time, threw her out of the mud single-handed.

An old informant tells me that Bill William, the first settler on Forrester's Point, ran off from a British warship, taking the name of Portland, after the peninsula in England, as a pseudonym. Of his marital life Richards (1953a:15) says . . .

> He married a full-blooded Esquimaux, and many
> are the stories told of the vicissitudes of this
> union. On one occasion Bill decided to get rid of
> his wife Hannah. He took her out in a boat, and
> was putting her overboard to drown her, when another
> boat came to the rescue. The occupants of the other
> boat, before intervening to save Hannah, called out,
> "what are you doing with your wife, Bill?" "Be gobs,
> Jack I'm goin' to get rid of her, boy. She's got me
> druv crazy." "But whose goin' to cook for you, and

mend your socks, and wash your clothes?" "Be gobs,
Jack, I did not think of that!" said Bill, and
forthwith pulled her into the boat again.

The first of the Newfoundlanders to settle in the area were Henry
Whalen of Brigus and John Carnell of Catalina. In the spring of 1850
they rounded the tip of the Great Northern Peninsula and sailed into the
Strait instead of following the usual summer fishery on the Labrador.[7]
Whalen became the first settler of Flowers Cove. Carnell and his family
left Flowers Cove after a short stay but after a few years returned
permanently (Richards 1953a, 1953b).[8] After this many of the immigrants
were Newfoundlanders together with some Jerseymen and Frenchmen. Many
of the Newfoundlanders and Jerseymen arriving after 1850 undoubtedly
came from the summer fishing stations that were established on the
Labrador side of the Strait. From the early marriage records (M.S.B.I.)
it can be seen that after 1850 most of the women coming into the area
were from eastern Newfoundland having probably come as stationers to the
Labrador side of the Strait.

An important factor in the settlement of the Strait was, of course,
the fishing rights of the French along the Treaty Shore.

> . . . Port au Choix was the first [French]
> fishing place [each summer]. After fishing at
> Port au Choix they would follow the fish to
> Ferolle Pt., then on to Flower's Cove and Savage
> Cove, and then across the Strait to Labrador
> (Richards, 1953b:23).

English settlement was officially forbidden, but, in the meager
historical material I have at my disposal, I have not found that their
settlement was prevented, or that they were harassed by the English navy
whose job it was to police the shore.

The French had the right to fish during the summer only and erect
on the shore only structures which pertained to the making of fish and
storing of gear. Relationships between the settlers and the French
seemed to have been usually good, and settlers were employed to watch and
care for the French structures and supplies left during the winter.
That some difficulties arose can be discerned in this incident quoted
from Richards (1953a:44) involving Big William.

> He [Big William] was employed by Genge to fish
> one half of the [Castor] river. French fishermen

CHART I

GENEOLOGY OF FIRST MARRIAGES

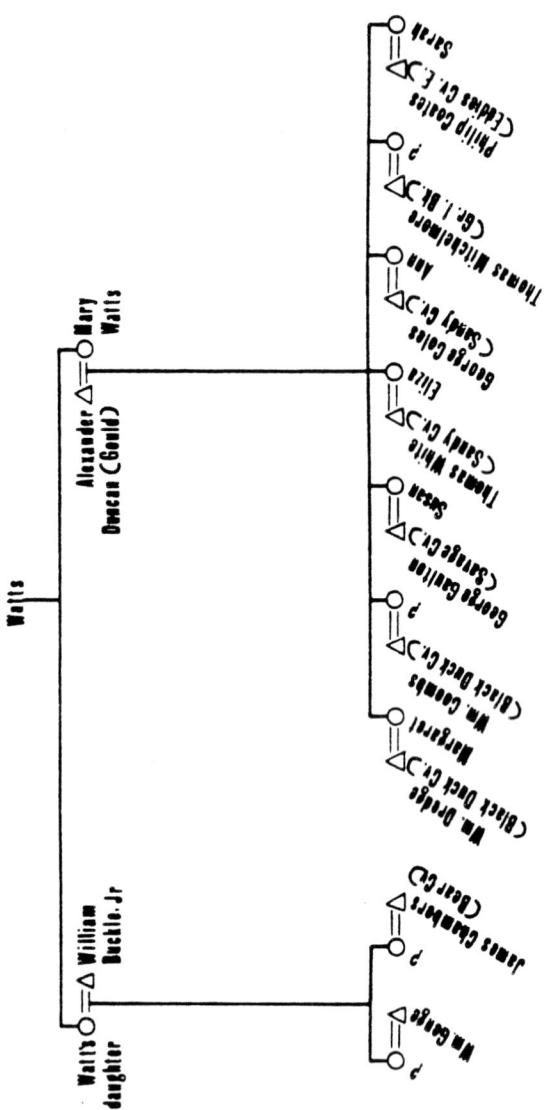

fished the other half. When the French warship
came Big William went to him [sic] requesting
that he be allowed to fish the whole river. The
result was that the French captain took the whole
river for the Frenchmen, and sent Uriah Eastman to
fish it. Big William met Eastman carrying his bed
up to his camp. An altercation took place, and he
gave him a tap under the chin and knocked him
unconscious. Afterwards, when recounting the
episode, Genge said to him, "What did you intend to
do with him, William?" He replied, "I wanted him
to straighten up so that I could put my left hand
under his rib and land him, bed and all out in the
river."

Also to be found in Richards (1953a:23) is this statement which
reflects a more understanding attitude on the part of the French.

I [the daughter of Henry Whalen] remember the
next year [1851] the harbour [Flower's Cove] filled
up with French brigs, and the French warship was
there. The captain came to father and said, "Don't
you know that you are catching our fish? You are
breaking the law!" The next day father did not go
fishing and the French captain said, "why are you
not out today, Whalen?" and father replied, "You
will not let me fish." The captain was a very kind
man, and said "you had better go on fishing, and I
will take care to be below when you come in, so
that I shall not see you."

The French had rights only on the Newfoundland shore, but none on
the Labrador, which was in the possession of Newfoundland (Toque, 1878:
258). On the Labrador side of the Strait hostility arose against the
French, and the local people who aided them, and against the Americans.

They say that they [certain planters and
stationers] are much disturbed by the French and
Americans. The former coming over from the other
side [of the Strait] in squadrons of batteaux,
sweeping all their best fishing grounds--while
the latter enter their harbours in schooners of
about 60 tons, catching their fish, and drying
them close to their own stages, which they
boldly assert they have a right to do by Treaty
(Toque, 1878:260-261).

Newfoundland and Jersey stationers established rooms on the
Labrador side of the Strait. Although individual settlers could establish
themselves on the Newfoundland side and work out a sub rosa existence,
large establishments with populations constantly moving between eastern

Newfoundland and Jersey could not.

It was some of the smaller Labrador fishermen who felt injured by the French coming across from the Newfoundland side and fishing the Labrador shore. It was claimed that in so doing the French depleted the supplies of cod and capelin and that this had resulted in the ruin of some of the fishermen. It was also claimed that some of the larger establishments profited by allowing the French to use their stages in return for the cod livers which were sold as oil (1878:261-262).

An illustration of such a complaint and a proof of the accuracy of Richards' approximation of the length of time the Genges had been in the area is found in the following:

> . . . the son of Mr. Grange [Genge], of Anchor
> Point, Newfoundland, came on board to complain
> that the French had stopped his father fishing a
> salmon river that has been in his family for up-
> wards of a century . . . (1878:268).

The above is attributed to a Captain Loch, probably the Captain of the British warship patrolling the coast in 1849. To give an idea of the size of the establishments on the Labrador side in 1849 we find that in Red Bay he says that there were . . .

> . . . thirteen rooms [establishments] . . .
> all belonging to separate planters, small
> proprietors, employing altogether 50 fishermen
> (exclusive of the shore-men), the principal
> person among them is a Mr. William Penny, of
> Conception Bay. He comes to this port in his
> schooner every spring, and arrived this year . . .
> with 95 people on board—forty men, the rest
> women and children. During the season there are
> about 100 inhabitants—40 reside for the purpose
> of seal-fishing during the winter (1878:260).

During the same year in Forteau Bay we find a larger operation proceeding. There were five planters employing around 400 individuals. Four of the establishments were connected with Jersey, Poole, and St. John's, while the fifth belonged to Mr. Grange [Genge], who was presented as being a "colonist" from Anchor Point, Newfoundland, and wealthy. "The most extensive planter on the coast of Labrador" was a Jerseyman, Mr. Philip de Quetteville. His operations in Forteau Bay and in Blanc Sablon were managed by Thomas Leroux, a Jersey merchant. De Quetteville "supplies most of the winter rooms and resident fishermen with goods, clothes, and stores much to his profit."

Blanc Sablon, "The principal fishing station on the Labrador Coast," contained four Jersey establishments and employed more than 300 people during the summer season, but only four families lived there during the winter (1878:260, 264-266).

> There are nine fishing stations between Red
> Bay and Forteau--namely, Carroll Cove--East St.
> Modeste--Black Bay--West St. Modeste--Captain
> [sic] Island--Lance Dialla--River head of Lance
> a Loup and Lance Amour. Except at Lance a Loup
> where a Mr. Crockwell, of Torquay, has a room,
> all these stations are fished by colonial
> fishermen, who send their product to St. John's
> by vessels from the port, and to the Jersey
> houses in Forteau Bay and Blanc Sablon (1878:
> 265).

Captain Loch approximated 220 men being employed in these latter small stations (1878:265).

Turnips and cabbages were grown at all of these Labrador fishing stations to be eaten during the summer. "Those who reside upon the coast during the winter shoot deer, partridges, ducks, geese, curlew, and other wild fowl, amply sufficient for their support." Traders from Quebec, Halifax and St. John's supplied them with port, flour, tea, and molasses. In Red Bay "The fishermen are paid principally in bills of exchange given by the merchants and receive from £18 to £25 a year," and men who worked only for the summer got half of their catch.

In Blanc Sablon "all the large establishments" payed their men £2 sterling a month (1878:261, 265, 267).

The larger settlements on the Labrador side of the Strait then, had quite an unstable population in contrast with those on the Newfoundland side as long as the stationer system lasted. In the latter the summer could find the arrival and departure of most of the population, but there were always the few permanent settlers who stayed on to become the ancestors of the present inhabitants.

On the Newfoundland shore, where there were no planters, with the exception of the Genges in the early days, the population was much more stable. Each cove was settled by a few families originally, and because of patrilocality and a lack of subsequent migration, these family names are still the only ones to be found. The population of Sandy Cove, for instance, with the exception of one man who has married in, consists entirely of Coles and Whites, whose settlement goes back at least to the early 1840's (M.S.B.I.).

A History of Settlement of Savage Cove

Savage Cove, being in no way Savage, is inappropriately named. The inhabitants are friendly and hospitable, and as the cove itself forms the first sheltered harbor south of Cape Norman, it cannot have anything to do with rough sea. That the name connotes barbarousness is unfortunate. Canadian and Newfoundland tourist leaflets often have lists of unusual Newfoundland place names, and Savage Cove is usually to be found among the forbidding ones.[9]

In her youth, one of the elderly ladies of the community had occasion to be alighting from the coastal boat as two men by the rail were discussing the implications of the name. One said, "Savage Cove-- must be savages who live here." "Well, here's one who's not!" replied the lady, and departed. When people from Savage Cove travel to southern parts of Newfoundland they sometimes say that they are from Flower's Cove. This is ostensibly because Flower's Cove is known whereas Savage Cove is not, but I have heard it said that people dislike the connotation of the name.

The first mention of the name is that of Ance aux Savage on a map of 1735, a copy of which is in the British Admiralty, Hydrographic Department, entitled A Chart of the Streights of Belisle, by G. Pelegrin (Seary, 1959:42; 1960:122). The name undoubtedly related to the following:

> Savage Cove is at the SW end of a track marked on some maps, which is virtually coterminous with the Straight Coast,[10] extending in a NW direction some 40 miles to Norman's Cove. The track is recorded [earliest] as: Passage des sauuages (Boissaic, 1669),[11] [and then variously as] . . . Passage of ye Savages . . . The Path of the Indians . . . [etc.]. . . It would seem to have been used by (?Montagnais) indians from the main-land of Labrador on their incursions into Newfound-land to avoid the harbourless stretch of the Straight Coast (Seary, 1960:123).

The first settler in Savage Cove was George Gaulton. He married Susan, one of Alexander Duncan's daughters. When Henry Whalen was going through the Straits in 1850, he entered Savage Cove, and seeing that it was a fine harbor, thought to settle down there, but was dissuaded by Gaulton. As Whalen's daughter, Elizabeth, tells it . . .

> After we anchored and went ashore, father said, "This seems like a fine harbor. I think we will settle here." Shortly after this old George Gaulton came around the harbour where we were. He was the first and only settler in Savage Cove at that time, and lived in the extreme south west corner. Father said to him, "I think we will settle down here, Mr. Gaulton." The old man got very angry, and said, "No you won't settle here. There is no room, no room." Savage Cove is a good mile around, and he was not in the real harbour at all. Then father walked to Flower's Cove, and went on a mile further to French Island Harbour. When he came back, he said, "We will go to French Island Harbour." Although Mr. Gaulton would not give consent for us to settle in Savage Cove, he was very glad to avail of the services of a mid-wife--Mrs. Noseworthy--who formed one of my party. That night a twin of boys was born to Mrs. Gaulton (Richards, 1953b:23).

In the same year Reverend Algernon Gifford, the first Anglican missionary in the area, inadvertently paid a visit to Savage Cove. He reports to Bishop Field in a letter. . . .

> On May 25th, the ice having opened in the Straits, I launches my boat under the pilotage of one of Mr. David's men, and set out for Anchor Point; but the tide being against us, we reached no nearer than Savage Cove, ten miles of my intended destination . . . here [is] a family of sixteen persons, two of whom are infants. There is not one of this large family who knows a letter of the alphabet[12] (1953b:23).

The north side of the harbor has been settled largely by Coles, Ways, and Hodges. There were two unrelated groups of Hodges in Savage Cove, but only one group remains today. Matthew Coles, the first Coles in Savage Cove, came from Sandy Cove and settled on the north side. He had nine sisters, one of whom married John Way, the first of his line to settle in Savage Cove, and another married William Hodge, the first of the second group of Hodges. These two settled on the north side also, and I have heard men on that side say "all our fathers were first cousins," as the present adult generation of Coles, Ways, and Hodges are all grandsons of these three brothers-in-law.

John Way came from Flower's Cove and William Hodge from Jersey via Blanc Sablon. His people were known as the "Jersey" Hodges to distinguish them from the others. This nickname also served to differentiate individuals who bore the same first and last names. These were distinguished in reference by prefixing their Christian names with "Jersey"; so there was "Jersey" George, and "Jersey" John.

When Matthew Coles arrived, John Way was already living on the north side as were the "non-Jersey" Hodges. The last of the latter moved to main brook about twenty years ago to work in the lumber woods in that area. There were Gaultons living on the south side when Coles arrived. The first Matchim probably arrived around that time, perhaps from Bonavista Bay, as he was the grandfather of all the present Matchims. He married a Gaulton and settled on the south side. There was also a family named Martin living there when Matthew Coles arrived, but they died out. A man named Tucker also lived on the point of land still known as Tucker's Point which project into the harbour on the south-east side, but he moved south of Reef's Harbour where his descendants live today.

In recent years the section of Savage Cove known locally as Charl't'on has developed on the ridge along the highroad above the southeast end of the cove. It is composed of families who once lived scattered on the south side of the cove plus others who have come in more recently. The Charl't'on houses form a compact group along the highroad, whereas the earlier homes on that side were spread well apart. This new area is also referred to as "the other side" by those living on the north side of the cove. The section was named in jest by a local wit after Charlestown, Prince Edward Island. The latter is considered locally to be a large sophisticated city, and as the inhabitants of the section in question are poor it was felt to be a jest to call them after the sophisticated town, of which Charl't'on is the local pronunciation.

The other settlements in the area tend to have persons with the same last name and of common patrilineal descent living in the same area of the community, but this is not considered to be a community division.

The Social Area

When culture-historians speak of a culture area they mean a geographical area containing peoples who share a similar culture content. We might speak, in the same fashion of a "social area" as a geographical area in which the inhabitants are all known to one another (share a similar "social context"). It is an area of maximum social interaction and may correspond to a geographical or political area. In this case the social area is "the Straits."[13]

The men in Savage Cove say that they know everyone to the northeast as far as Eddies Cove East, 13 miles away. To the southwest the approximation varies, some men will say that they know everyone as far as Anchor Point, 11 miles away, and some say as far as Ferrole, 28 miles away. By this is meant, not that every individual is known, but that all the adult men are known and many of the adult women. Until recently one did not come to know many people in other settlements until one grew up and started travelling about, but now with communication facilitated by the road, and by the opening of the high school in Flower's Cove, the adults say that the children of different settlements become acquainted in a way that they never previously did.

The extent of the social area related to population distribution. Eddies Cove is the last settlement to the northeast before one encounters the Straight Coast which is uninhabited, except for Big Brook, thirteen miles away, and the settlements are fairly close and continuous to the southwest until one reaches Ferolle after which the population thins considerably. Although the people in Big Brook are known they are not usually cited in the responses people give regarding the area of their acquaintance. They tend to do their shopping in Cook's Harbor to the northeast, rather than in Flower's Cove and hence they are not often in the area.

What is most important is not how far people are actually known, or whether all men are actually known, but that the area is conceived as one in which such familiarity exists. Such a conception supplies us with a local orientational unit that is greater than the settlement. Individuals and relatives are known, of course, beyond this area of maximum social interaction. People are known to the northeast in Boat Harbor, Cooks Harbor, and around the tip of the Peninsula in St. Anthony and Main Brook. To the southwest beyond Anchor Point or Ferolle knowledge of individuals fades. Some have friends and relatives in Deer Lake, Corner Brook, and St. John's, and some know people on the mainland. Certain friends and relatives also exist on the adjacent Labrador, and these relationships are maintained in the summer time when the men go there to fish.

The fact that there is no settlement other than on the coast in this area[14] has its influence on the "shape" of the social area.

The social area is also marked off conceptually by reference to outside areas and groups. "The French Shore" is locally conceived to run east from Cook's Harbor (or northeast from Big Brook) and down the eastern side of the Peninsula. A reason given for that area being called "The French Shore" is the place names of French derivation that are found there. Although this area is only part of what was once the French Shore, which extended to Cape Ray, it roughly corresponds to the statement of James (1937:I, 51) that,

> "The French Shore" is from Cape St. John to the
> Straits of Belle Isle, so called because French
> fishermen up to 1903 held fishing rights on this and
> other parts of the coast."

Anecdotes are told about this area concerning collisions between dog teams. According to the men of Savage Cove, the commands to turn right and left are reversed from Cook's Harbor eastward. When a team from the Straits comes together with a team from the latter area, each carter calls out to his "head" dog to keep to the right so the teams can pass. However, if one or both of the head dogs hears and obeys the command intended for the other the teams will collide as that command will indicate "turn left" to the other team.

People have heard of the jack-a-tars,[15] French speaking Newfound-landers living on the Port-au-Port Peninsula and in a few other areas in the southwestern part of the island. They are also aware of the different accent of the people of St. George's Bay, south of the Port-au-Port Peninsula, as well as some of the other accents of southern and eastern Newfoundland.[16] People are acquainted with the French speakers across the Strait on the Quebec Labrador. A few come to Savage Cove in the summer to buy lumber.

Another grouping to be considered are the <u>townies</u>, the town dwellers. The people of St. John's have always considered all other Newfoundland communities <u>outports</u>.

Some rural Newfoundlanders feel that there are urbanites who look down upon them. Now, with their recent growth, Grand Falls, Deer Lake, and Corner Brook are taking on the characteristics of towns. Men from the Straits wearing seal skin boots in Corner Brook find that children call <u>skinny-hoppers</u> after them, and outporters in St. John's are taunted with <u>bay-noddy</u> and <u>bay-wop</u>. To many townies outporters in the north are adulterous, although this is not in fact the case in the Straits, while the outporters are shocked by what they consider to be the great amount of crime and desertion in the towns.

The people of the Straits have been influenced by the Eskimos in that they have taken over various items of Eskimo clothing such as seal skin boots, skin mittens, and cloth parkas called <u>dickies</u> or <u>kazaks</u>. Men's home knit sweaters are decorated with a double line at the bottom and at the cuffs which remind one of the similar decoration which is typical of Eskimo clothing. The entire Eskimo dog traction complex has also been taken over, and there is at least one Eskimo myth that has been adapted as a local saying. How and when these items were incorporated is unknown.

The social area is marked by intimacy and informality. When individuals from within the area meet they interact as friends rather than as strangers. People are free to visit each other's houses uninvited, and they walk right into the kitchen without knocking when they do so. Only a stranger knocks in this part of Newfoundland. "If you went clear of this shore you'd knock then, but you wouldn't knock at any house on this shore." Knocking is a ritual in which the outsider's strangeness is announced. The kitchens of the settlements are always open, but visitors do not enter the rest of the house without invitation. The charter for such activity is "Around here you goes where you likes and does what you wants." Here the open house goes with the closed community. Since all who are in the area are relatives or acquaintances, there are no strangers to be kept out.

This does not mean, of course, that people do go anywhere they like any time they like. Visiting, as all interaction, is governed by friend-

ship, kinship, contractual relations, and contiguity, but still the
ethic endures and reflects social reality to a great extent. To say
that "Around here you does what you wants," does not mean that there
are no restrictions upon the individual, but implies that (1) because
of their extensive personal relations people don't suffer the
restrictions that they feel would be placed upon them in an impersonal
urban society, and (2) social sanctions are largely informal.

There are several factors involved in the "maintenance" of the
social area. First, of course, we have a small population derived
largely from different settlements. Until recently most men in the area
worked in the lumber woods during the fall. There were local company
camps which took men from the entire area who then got to know each other.
During the summer the men of the Newfoundland shore of the Strait fish
on the Labrador side during the last part of the fishing season, and
there they interact with the settlers on that shore. The latter are
said to be very friendly towards them, despite the fact they crowd
their working spaces and compete with them for their catch.

Another factor is the hospitality shown to travellers. People
say that before the road was completed in November 1962 a man would
travel on until night overtook him and then would proceed to the nearest
house where he would be given a lunch and a place to stay for the night.
I was told that once a party of ten men were received at a house one
night. They were told by the host that there were no beds for all of them
to sleep in, but they could sleep on the kitchen floor and keep the fire
in during the night. This type of hospitality has an economic base
in the lack of cash and facilities that exist in the area, but it is
also a social obligation that would be reciprocated, plus yielding
news and a chance for different, interesting companionship.

The antithesis of the member of local society is the stranger.
This is a person who has no place in local society, and because he is
unknown his behavior is unpredictable. Since the highroad connecting
the area with the rest of Newfoundland to the south was finished, there
have been a good many more strangers in the area. Before this the main
transportation in and out of the area was by coastal steamer and these do
not run from January to June due to the ice. However, about five years
ago the road was opened to St. Anthony, breaking down isolation somewhat

and in recent years, until the road to the south was put through, it was
possible to go in and out on the bi-weekly mail plane which landed at
Flower's Cove. People are somewhat apprehensive about the new road,
saying that strangers could come in on the road from anywhere and can do
anything and be gone. They say that in the past there was no crime
locally because you could not hope to get away with anything as everyone knew each other so well. That people are apprehensive about
strangers does not mean that they are cold or unkind to them. On the
contrary, people are quite friendly to the outsider and are often quite
eager to establish relationships. A man once remarked to me that when
the road was first opened people were concerned about who might be
coming through, but when they met the outsiders they found that they were
just like themselves.

The archetype of the stranger is the Runaway. He is a fantasy
figure of whom children and women out berry picking are afraid. He is
thought of as running away from somebody or something, is dangerous, and
may be carrying a gun. This image is based upon the runaways that
actually did exist in the past. Some of the ancestors of the people in
the area did run away from British and French ships, and there are at
least two old men living on the Peninsula today who ran off from French
fishing boats. Conditions aboard the latter were very hard and punish-
ments severe, and many aboard the British warships were impressed seamen.

However, the real runaways were readily and easily incorporated
into local society. People took them in and gave them work, and they
and their offspring married into local society. A parallel exists in
attitudes towards strangers today. People are apprehensive about them,
but once they are encountered they are courteously negotiated with.[17]
Children are threatened with strangers, their parents saying that they
will take them away if they are not good. Children are also afraid of
runaways, and are afraid of and threatened with Santa Clause, the Boo Man,
the Nurse (at the Grenfell Nursing Station), the Mounties (RCMP), and
Christmas mummers. Such figures have the latent function of deflecting
hostility of children away from their disciplining parents and displacing
the generally acquired hostility of adults.[18] Children are not threatened
with punishment by these various figures but they are threatened that
they will be taken away by them, thus reflecting the security felt in
the family and in-group, and the insecurity in the outside and unknown.

Another factor making for commonality within the area is religion. Most people are Church of England, although there have long been some Roman Catholic and United Church members in the area. There are also some Pentecostals in Nameless Cove, and in Big Brook, just outside the social area, whose inhabitants came from Nameless Cove. In 1849 the Anglican Mission of the Strait of Belle Isle was established with Algernon Gifford as the first missionary priest. The mission at that time had its headquarters in Forteau and included communities on both sides of the Strait (Toque, 1878:284). Mr. Gifford was presented to his mission by Bishop Field with whom he travelled during the latter's visit. It is said that the boundary of the Newfoundland Labrador at Blanc Sablon was "the first limit or end of his Diocese that his Lordship had ever seen" (1878:254). The early missionary priests were members of the Society for the Propagation of the Gospel in Foreign Parts. Missionaries have included J. J. Curling, after whom the town of Curling (in the southwest part of the island) was named, and Canon J. T. Richards.

Today, the mission headquarters is at Flower's Cove, where stands St. Barnabas Church. This church is known locally as "skin boot" church, because the money to erect it was obtained by the sale of seal skin boots made by the women of the mission. Up until about 15 years ago almost everyone wore seal skin boots, and women would be up until the small hours of the night sewing and tapping boots for the use of their own families. As the boots manufactured for the mission were done in addition to this the labor involved was no small contribution.

St. Barnabas Church is considered to belong to the people of the entire mission, even though each community has its own small church at which services are held when the priest visits and when lay readers are available. The people of the mission try to attend Christmas and Easter services at St. Barnabas which is crowded to overflowing on these occasions.

There is little religious conflict in the area, although Newfoundland as a whole had had its share of religious dissension. It is said that "around here people aren't dirty about religion." A live and let-live attitude is maintained as far as the three previously established religions, Anglican, Roman Catholic, and United are concerned. However,

some irritation is displayed regarding the local evangelican group due
to their active proselytizing. 'They're always telling you that your
religion is no good and that you're going to Hell."

The religious tolerance in the area is illustrated by the lack
of concern regarding marriage between Anglicans, Roman Catholics, and
United Church. In accordance with the patriarchial, patrilocal family
system it is assumed that the woman in such circumstances will
automatically adopt her husband's religion. This is deemed to be the
best arrangement for all as it makes for harmony in the home. The shift
of allegiance on the part of the woman is quite automatic and often there
is no discussion of it before the marriage.

The fact that the area is preponderantly of a single faith is
related to the lack of tension, as there are not enough members of
minor groups to pose a threat. There is but one United Church and one
Roman Catholic Church in the area, both in Flower's Cove. A Pentecostal
Church is now being built in Nameless Cove. In the past there was some
anti-Roman Catholic feeling and some men were said to be afraid to spend
the night in a Roman Catholic community.

There are two Anglican social organizations in the Straits. The
men's organization is the Orange Lodge and the women's organization is
the CEWA (Church of England Women's Association). There are Orange Lodge
buildings only at Green Island Brook and Flower's Cove and the
organization is not as active as it was in the past--no men from Savage
Cove belong. Although this organization has an anti-Catholic orientation,
it does not seem to be militant. The Lodges put on times periodically.
There is a CEWA in each community and it has an active role in community
life. The women of this organization put on times during which they raise
money for the settlement school and church and for contributions to
general church funds. Times attract people from a wide area. In order
to be a success a time must gather a great many people to it from outside
the community for economic as well as social reasons, because in order
to make all the effort that has gone into their preparation worth while
a fairly substantial amount of money must be collected and this is
dependent upon attendance.

Socials are held in the community school houses. For the children
there is homemade ice cream for five cents a cone and jigs [grab bag

prizes] for five cents each. For the adults there is a raffle. "Baskets"
containing items that would appeal to men, such as cigarettes, cookies,
tinned fruit, are auctioned off. Small articles are hung "on the line."
Here, things that appeal to the women, aprons, towels, and so forth, are
pinned to a clothesline for display and sale. The main entertainment is
square dancing usually with an accordian accompaniment. Today the dance
is most often a "cotillion" (with the accent upon the first syllable)
although another square dance form called "sets" is sometimes performed.
Individual men will often step-dance. The time is not limited to the
school house, as the men will go to nearby houses to drink, step-dance
and sing.

Attendance at times is decreasing due to the presence of
restaurants. The only restaurant in the area which serves regular
meals is in Flower's Cove. Aside from this Flower's Cove has a few
snack-bar-recreation establishments called restaurants and there is one
in Savage Cove. Here cokes, "chips," bars, fried chicken legs, hot-dogs,
hamburgers and ice cream are served. There are juke boxes, snooker type
games, and in two of the restaurants (one in Flower's Cove and the other
in Savage Cove) movies are shown regularly. The presence of restaurants
as recreational centers has cut down on some of the entertaining that
was previously done in the homes, as well as attendance at times. In
Savage Cove attendance at times suffers because they are always held on
Friday, which is one of the bi-weekly movie nights.[19] Another recreation
which attracts people from the entire area is the concert. This is an
amateur theatrical consisting of skits and songs. They were usually
church-sponsored but in recent years the Girl Guides have also "put
them off."

Visiting is not as extensive as it used to be. People did more
cruising in the past, and women might take children and make extensive
trips to other communities, staying with relatives and friends.

Ties between settlements in the social area are also maintained
through marriage. The residence pattern is patrilocal with men marrying
women from both within and without the settlement. About half of the
wives in Savage Cove are from outside the community, but all are from
the Straits. As men tend to remain in the communities in which they
were born and work with their agnates they form patrilocal extended

families which are often connected by marriage to similar families in other communities.

As previously mentioned there were no merchants in the Strait before World War I except at Flower's Cove. Although there are now merchants in other settlements most of the larger merchants and the regional co-operative are located in Flower's Cove. This means that people of the area shop regionally and have most of their economic contacts in the area.

> Flower's Cove has developed as a strong regional capital for 25 miles of coast between Current Island on the south and Eddies Cove East on the north. The most important supplier of goods in this area is the Flower's Cove Co-operative Society, established in 1948. This large shop is well stocked with every line of goods including such things as hardware, clothing, and bulk building supplies. Most of these goods come directly to Flower's Cove from the manufacturers in Toronto, Montreal, and the Maritimes-- by C.N.R. boat and by schooner; other goods come up by truck from Corner Brook. Before the new highway came through, the residents in the hinterland of this Society came by boat, horse, dog-team, and snow-mobile to pick up their supplies; now, small shops have opened in most of the surrounding communities, and the store owner goes to Flower's Cove by pick-up truck to collect his goods.
>
> The new highway, however, completed late in 1962, has attracted two truckers along this coast. Whereas in the other two study areas, these trucks were acting as wholesalers, these are merely acting as haulage agents, picking up orders already placed with whole-salers in Corner Brook and moving them north to the shops on the coast. This has allowed a number of small shops to open up in areas previously dominated commercially by Flower's Cove. These trucks are supplying--to a greater or lesser extent--all the settlements that can be reached by road as far north as Eddies Cove East. The Cook's Harbour area continues to get its supplies by schooner and C.N.R. (Head, 1963: 178).

The Equalitarian Community

Society in the Straits is basically equalitarian. This of course, does not mean that there are no differences in wealth and prestige--far from it. Yet, even differences in wealth are not great, and the outward display of such differences as exist is not extensive. All men are not, however, considered as being of equal worth. The industrious, hard worker who makes something of himself, especially if he betters himself from a very humble beginning, is considered more of a man than others, and those who are irresponsible and lazy are considered somewhat childish.

Despite these considerations, the dominant ethic is that of equality. No man's doors are closed to another and each is received much as the other, with friendliness and camaraderie. One gets the feeling that the men act as if they were shipmates together on the same cruise, and though there are certainly differences in the ways in which people regard each other, it is best to let these bide under a feeling of general good will and acceptance.

The feelings of men for their fellows are reflected in terms of address. In speaking to one another men most frequently address each other as boy, and slightly less frequently, my son. A less common, but still frequently heard form is my dear, and my love and my doll are heard occasionally. The latter two are more used by men when speaking to children. Sir and skipper are used when addressing strangers, though sir is sometimes used by men who are known to one another when meeting. Skipper is also used to designate the head of the household or crew. Mr. is used when speaking to the school teacher or the parson.

As males are generally "boys," women are generally "maids." Maid, and rarely my maid, is the general term of address towards women. Little girls, unmarried and married women are all addressed as maid.[20] Females address men as boy and my dear, but not usually my son--only when they are a generation above the man, or for emphasis. Women are addressed as maid by men as well as women. My dear is also used by both men and women in addressing women, but is not used quite as frequently as maid.

People are addressed as Uncle and Aunt when they become "oldish." This is usually sometime after fifty. These are said to be terms of respect. Mr. and Mrs. would be too formal and to call them by the more informal terms, or by their first names only would be disrespectful. Uncle may be used as a term of respect to a prestigious outsider who is younger.

Terms of address, then, mirror the intimacy and egalitarian nature of social life in the area. All males in the social area (with the exception of one's father and grandfathers), are <u>boy</u>, or <u>uncle</u>. All females (except one's mother and grandmothers) are <u>maid</u> or <u>aunt</u>. This, aside from the sexual division, cleaves the social world into a group of peers and a group of honoured elders. There still is another differentiation however, in that the dead are always referred to as <u>poor</u> as for instance, poor Uncle John, or poor Aunt Jane.

The exceptions to this usage inside the social area are those who are called <u>Mr.</u>; whereas those outside the area are <u>skipper</u>, <u>sir</u>, <u>Mr.</u>, or <u>buddy</u>. <u>Buddy</u> is used to refer to an unknown person, or generally to refer to the other fellow, and in relating an incident a person might say, "Then buddy said . . . ," or "Buddy did (thus and so on)."

Combinations of terms can be used to designate, for instance, recognition of separate status and intimacy as when I was addressed as "Mr. Firestone, boy," or "Mr. Firestone, my son." In the same way, my wife was sometimes addressed as "Mrs. Firestone, Sharon." On the other hand, recognition of higher status and strangeness was indicated when I was once addressed by an oldish man as "uncle buddy."

Also consonant with local egalitarianism is that in essence there is only one occupational status for men and one for women. All women are housewives, and men are basically fishermen, though they gain a living from the land and sea in various combinations of ways-- but these ways do not distinguish them. Almost all men in this area fish and before the company camps closed down most men cut wood during the fall. Men also hunt to supply their own tables and for sport; there are very few men in the Straits who only trap, but in the past there was more trapping. Many men walk over the ice after seals in the spring. When the lumber camps were open most men would fish during the summer and go into the woods during the fall. So, there is no one occupation that has become associated with any type of character or position in contrast with any other. A man does what he must to get a living, given the exigencies of life. One does not find "the Fisherman" in contrast with "the Logger," in contrast with "the Hunter." Each man has done all these things and few do only one for a living. Even the merchant is only a partial exception to this, for most of the merchants in the area either fish themselves or have brothers who cooperate with

them and fish. And although merchants have higher prestige than most
men, and most of the political authority, they still come within the
general category of men of the area. The main exceptions to this are
the school teachers, and the priests. These are almost always men
from the outside area anyway, and are always addressed as Mr. This
status tends to endure. A man came to Savage Cove several years ago
to teach, married a local girl, and settled down fishing. He now
teaches outside the community. He is still addressed as Mr. There is
some feeling that teachers are not as strong and capable at the local
jobs as the men are themselves. This is so despite the fact that most
of the teachers coming in are from outports and have done all these
traditional jobs. Only the jackets made for teachers and women have
tassels decorating them.

The same situation applies even more strongly to women. There is
but one status, that of housewife. The exceptions to this are the
female school teacher and nurse, the latter is always addressed as
Miss. The former may be, but her position is not that divorced from
the women in the community in general.

The attitude of equality is reflected in the gregariousness
and good fellowship that is to be found when men get together to talk,
sing, drink or play cards. Late adolescents and more mature men
interact as equals at times and weddings.

In the Straits, then, one is either a member of local society,
a specialist from the outside who is working in the area (teacher,
nurse, etc.), or a stranger. As people are used to having a personal
knowledge of everyone in the area the stranger is a special person. He
is a special person because people are not used to dealing with
individuals they do not know. They are not practiced in impersonal
relationships. There is, no "ethic of impersonality," as is found in
more urbanized areas.

In cities the vast majority of people one sees everyday, perhaps
without meaningfully perceiving them, are strangers and there is an
ideal expected pattern of behavior for dealing with them. One is
expected to be impersonal, somewhat informal, and reasonably polite
with the understanding that the encounter is of a limited duration and

for the purpose of some particular end (this would be true even of a conversation of strangers on a train)--and that only a very limited aspect of the total personality of the individual is involved. How unknown people are dealt with in urban areas can, of course, vary in quality from, perhaps treating them as "non-persons" in Goffman's sense (1959:43) to, at best, behavior in the manner of a genuine "service with a smile." At any rate, there are techniques for dealing with strangers and they are not conceived of as significant figures, as such. However, this is seen only when contrasting the urban with the rural scene.

The changes that have been taking place in recent years are altering the nature of the intimacy within the social area. Up until about 30 years ago many people would go into the woods to live during the winter. Several families from Savage Cove would do this, and their little community in the country was jokingly called Savage Cove. Flower's Cove had a winter community called L'Anch, three miles inland, and the people of Anchor Point moved to a nearby sheltered inlet for the winter. Some settlements on the Labrador still have a separate winter residence. The Savage Cove winter quarters consisted of small, rough shacks with bunk beds for the children. These are remembered as cozy and warm. One woman said that she remembered it as like a snow scene on a Christmas card.

One reason for the winter move was that one was away from the wind and consequently much of the cold, on the exposed coast. There are no trees around the settlements and the wind can blow very strong for days at a time. Another reason for the move was that the men could cut wood for nearby lumber camps and not have to be too far from their families. When education became mandatory, the winter move could not be made as the children had to remain in school.

The Canon Richards Memorial High School also affected relations within the area when it was built in Flower's Cove. Children from the entire area now are taken by bus to Flower's Cove to attend high school, and this has made for changes. I have heard complaints that girls are beginning to smoke, an activity which is taboo for women in the area, and even to use bad language. It is said this is because they form a group at the high school and reinforce their beliefs that these things are all right. Therefore, the high school has meant the establishment of a new reference group, and one that is making for the ready acceptance of outside styles.

This change is seen ultimately as the result of the highroad. If it weren't for the highroad the high school could not have opened as there would have been no way of transporting the children from the various communities. In the same way the road is another source of worry to parents as they say that children will get into cars with people they do not know. This situation is the obverse of fear of strangers on the child's part because anyone usually in the social area is expected to belong there.

CHAPTER III

THE PATRILOCAL EXTENDED FAMILY

The major feature of social structure in the Straits is the patrilocal
extended family, which also constitutes the primary economic group, the
fishing crew. The extended family holds property, controls production,
distribution, and inheritance. Such a group contains nuclear families
as domestic groups, and goes through a regular process of fussion. The
rites of passage, birth, death, and marriage, are rituals that pertain
particularly to the nuclear family.

The Structure of Crews

The family which inhabits a house is ideally a part of a larger
group, the patrilocal extended family. When brothers grow up they are
expected to fish with each other and their father. After the father dies
the oldest brother becomes the leader, and the group may be referred to
by his name ("Jack's crew") just as it was considered to be his father's
when he was living. When the brothers' children grow up there will in
most cases be a split and each brother will fish with his sons. This
group is referred to as a crowd or crew.[1] The head of this group is the
skipper.[2]

These terms have not only an immediate reference to the work group
but a larger symbolism. They are literally descriptive in that the head
of the patrilocal extended family is the director of fishing operations
and boat handling, in which the men of this group operate under his
direction. The terms also symbolize a family structure of superordinate
and subordinate relationships as well as relationships of equality among
members. That is, the father, or in his stead the eldest brother, is
the leader and director in all affairs of the group and is superior, too,
in authority and prestige. On the other hand, the brothers, or junior
brothers if the father is deceased, are in general behavior always a
group of equal partners under the authority of the skipper.

The crew has a company account with the local merchant. That is,
all purchases which pertain to the group as a whole are charged to that
account which the group has under its company[3] name. Such names are
still to be seen on some trucks and snowmobiles as until recently it was
mandatory by law that they display the owner's name. Thus a truck might

bear the name of, say, "John Smith and Sons," and this would not refer
to a commercial company, but to the company represented by the patrilocal
extended family. In those few instances where adult brothers have not
"split up" after their sons have grown up and are fishing with them, a
sign such as "John Smith & Bros. & Sons" might be seen.

There are, however, other company accounts than those which are
maintained by the family. Whenever men who are not all members of the
same extended family come together in a joint venture they form a company
for that purpose and open an account with a merchant to which all purchases
pertaining to that venture will be charged. The account will carry the
name of one of the men involved, such as John Smith & Company. After
the activity has run its course for that season, the men pay off this
account with their earnings and then split the remainder equally among
themselves. If, for instance, the task is sealing, the gasoline for the
boats' engines and other expenses are charged to the company account, and
after the pelts have been sold the bill to the merchant is paid and all
hands share evenly in the profit.

Aside from sealing, activities which most often foster such accounts
are lumbering (chopping and sawing wood for lumber rather than the cutting
of pulp wood) and fishing on the Labrador side of the Strait after the
bait (capelin) has left the Newfoundland side. In many cases all and
only the men of the extended family engage together in these activities
as well as in fishing on the Newfoundland side of the Strait, the latter
being the primary economic activity engaged in by the crew. Sometimes
other individuals will join a crew, say, for fishing on the Labrador, or
two crews might go in together in lumbering. Moreover, individuals
rather than an entire crew or crews may come together for sealing or
Labrador fishing. A man, then, may be involved in various company accounts,
the most permanent of which is that of his crew--that is, his extended
family.

Aside from the company account which serves the entire crew,
each married man has his own account to which all his household expenses
are charged. It does not matter how many children each brother has in
his family, he gets but his single share. Thus, equal division among all
adult brothers and their father is considered the basic economic arrangement. This may at times lead to dissension, discussed below, but usually

endures even in unusual circumstances. For instance, in one crew where
one of the brothers has steady employment in another part of the province
his brothers each take for themselves out of the company account only
the amount of his salary. In this way it is felt he keeps his share of
the company even though absent as all brothers are sharing alike in their
combined ventures. In another crew a brother who is permanently employed
elsewhere and will probably never return to fish is considered to have
his share in the company in theory but not in actuality.

The company account reflects the economic relationship that
existed in Newfoundland between fishermen and merchants. There has in
the past been little cash or capital in the possession of the fishermen,
and traditionally they have been fitted out by the local merchants.
The merchant supplied the fisherman at the beginning of the season with
the materials that he needed for fishing and with food. At the end of
the season the merchant took the catch of the fisherman to recompense
him for what he had laid out, and paid the fisherman the difference.
In the past when the price of fish was low, fishermen were sometimes in
perpetual debt under this system as the amount they got for their fish
could be less than the cost of their yearly fitting out. Now, as the
economic situation has improved, most fishermen are out of debt. In the
past it was almost a necessity that the fishermen sell their catch to
the merchant who fitted them out. However, as they are now out of debt
to him and so do not feel obligated to sell him their catch, they may
sell to the cooperative in Flower's Cove or itinerant agents--outlets
which are relatively new.

At the present time even those crews that have sufficient cash to
pay for their own fishing supplies at the beginning of the season continue
to be fitted out by a merchant because it provides a convenient accounting
system--individual purchases made for the group are merely added to the
account and settled up at the end of the season. Few families are now
fitted out with food.

A great economic advantage of the patrilocal extended family is
that by means of it a group of men can pool their resources to obtain
capital goods. Economically the individuals involved have "more power."
It would be difficult for one man to purchase trucks, snowmobiles and
outboard motors, and this to a lesser degree is also true of the more
traditional items such as boats, nets, and other fishing equipment.

The most important economic implication of this type of family structure is that it provides the number of men necessary for efficient fishing. For trap fishing one needs a number of men, and a group comprised of a man with a few grown sons is about the right size. Men who have no grown sons and no brothers accordingly have difficulty as it is hard not only to fish efficiently but to keep up the requisite gear without year around adult help. Sharemen may be employed for the fishing season, but, although some are quite conscientious and skilled, many are felt to be unsatisfactory in not taking an interest in the upkeep of the equipment, and they are not on hand the year around to attend to the various tasks that need doing. Sharemen get one half of one share of the catch and their room and board during the fishing season. They provide no gear.

Aside from this, when there are many men in a crew there are more who can go out and obtain employment in other places during the non-fishing season. Until the last few years most men worked in the woods during the fall cutting pulp wood. It would not be easy for a man alone to leave and go into the woods, but a man's sons could after the fish was made, or some might go while it was being made if there had been a light catch, and this would be an added source of revenue. The more hands there are, the more can go to seek temporary employment when times are bad. When contemplating the results of a year in which there was a slim catch a man said, "The young men will just have to go out." Also, since the tasks that are to be done are so numerous, ranging from boat building and house building, to care of automobiles and snowmobiles, the more individuals about and helping, the more easily these jobs are done.

In the past there were many extended families that had no household accounts. There was but the company account and to this were charged all the food, clothing and other articles purchased by the father for the group, as well as the fishing supplies. Where there are individual household accounts only fishing supplies are laid to the company account.

Where there was only the company account, food would be stocked in a communal store and shared by all the households. They would all "eat out of one flour barrel," both in the sense that they shared what had been purchased for all and, literally, in that the family head would open a barrel of flour which all would use until the contents were consumed.

51

> With my father and certain other people of his
> time only the old man had an account. You passed
> all the money you made over to him, even after you
> were married, and he would buy for the grub store
> for everybody. We all ate out of one flour barrel.
> He would give us [the sons] spending money whenever
> we wanted it.

This type of single account system is rare today, but was common
a generation ago.

Sons hand over to their fathers all outside income, such as money
earned cutting pulpwood, in both systems, but where there are household
accounts each son gets his cash portion of the group's income when he
marries. This is done at least by the time he builds his house and
"shifts out" for himself, which, in most cases, is as soon as he can.
In order to do this he must have his own household account. If he has
an actual share in the company at this time (if he is in a three
generation family) he will be receiving an equal portion with his
brothers and/or father. If he has no actual share in the company at
this time (if he is in a four generation family) he will be receiving an
equal portion with his brothers in the share which his father owns in
the company—the other shares being held each by his father's brothers
and perhaps also by his father's father, if the latter is still alive.
This will be further described later on. The rationale for household
accounts is that without them those brothers having few children are
penalized, as much of their efforts are going into providing for their
brothers' children.

Brothers and their father remaining together and "all hauling
together" is the ideal. After the father dies the brothers should stay
together until their boys have grown up. Then the brothers split up.
There are, however, instances where first cousins do fish together, and
this was more prevalent in the past. In the first instance, where
cousins do not work together, we have an extended family lasting but
three generations and including the founder, his sons and their immature
children. In the latter, where cousins cooperate within a single crew,
we have a family extending over four generations and including the
founder, his sons, grandsons, and their immature off-spring. Unless
otherwise stated the generalizations that follow refer specifically to
the three generation family.

If men split up before their boys are grown "people talk about it." A woman who married into tne settlement from a nearby community said that one of the things that upset her mother a great deal was that her sons did not work together after their father died. She felt that if the father had lived longer until they had accumulated more gear they would have kept together, and she worried about any quarrels that arose between them. Men are reticent to split up because they feel that "people will think that we can't agree," but one reason for their splitting up is precisely that: a man may be willing to take orders from his father but not from his older brother. Ordinarily, the members of crews work together in harmony despite the rivalry and competition expressed not only between crews but between individuals in crews.

I have heard it said that a woman may provoke a split by complaining to her husband that he is either bearing an undue amount of the labor or not receiving an appropriate share of the profits. There is greater danger of this occurring where there are no household accounts and the father handles the money and doles it out to the sons.

Another factor leading to the premature break-up of crews is the differential in numbers of children. As mentioned previously earnings are split in equal share among all the brothers regardless of the number of their children. As both boys and girls help in very important ways during the fishing season the fact that one brother may have few children helping while another has many children helping may be felt to be unfair. This is likely to be more of an issue in very small crews where the importance of children assisting is much greater.

A more serious problem occurs where a son of one of the brothers is mature and able enough to do a man's share of the work while his cousins are not. Bad feeling may arise from such a situation as the boy's family may feel that as he is doing a man's share of the work, in contrast with the smaller contribution of his uncle's boys, he is entitled to some part of the actual profits. Although he will have an equal share with his brothers in his father's share of the company after his father and his uncles split he has no share in the crew at that time and as such receives only what his father sees fit to give him out of his own share.

Where such an "imbalance" is not redressed the resulting

disagreement may provoke a split. If the brothers who have shares in the company have roughly the same number of boys who have come to maturity fairly evenly no special arrangements have to be made.

The following is an example of a situation in which the labor provided by those holding shares was quite disproportionate. There were two brothers in the area who fished together, but whereas one had a number of adult sons, the other had none. Nonetheless, each received his half and no provision was made for the labor of the mature sons. This situation persisted for a number of years during which the brother having the sons was apparently satisfied. However, a split eventually took place after which he complained about the many years during which his boys had not gotten their proper share.

The usual way this problem is solved is by giving the mature son a half share, or, in other words, taking him on at the same rate as a shareman. In such cases an extra full share is made, one half of which goes to the son, and the other half is divided equally among all the brothers, including the boy's father.

It has occurred, but only rarely, that a son will receive a full share with his father and uncles. Such a case occurred in a nearby community. There were two brothers one of whom had no sons and the other had only one who, when grown, had a full share. In another case a son was to have gotten a full share in a crew composed of his father, uncles and their first cousins, but he left the settlement before this took place when a good job opening arose elsewhere. Here the father had put in twice his own share towards the maintenance of the crew's gear for that coming season's fishing and the boy may have previously contributed towards some of the capital equipment owned by the company. Also, the father, the eldest of his brothers, had contributed greatly to their support before they had grown up, and the father and his brothers had given equal shares in the past to their first cousins, who had joined the crew, before they had a cod trap of their own and all were using the trap of the father and uncles. These factors undoubtedly contributed toward the son obtaining a full share. Ordinarily, it would not be considered fair to the shareholders since they had worked in the crew and maintained it all their lives but now would have no greater share in it than their nephew who was buying in.

A mature son being taken on on the same basis as a shareman is only a temporary measure. It means only an additional income, he still owns only his one potential share in the crew that his father would head should a split occur. When it does, or when increasing maturity evens out the work load in the crew, this special status ceases. In those rare instances where a son receives a full share with his father and uncles the inheritance pattern would be altered. Local speculation on such a hypothetical inheritance includes the suggestion that such a son would also be entitled to his normal inheritance of one part of his father's share as well as his full share. This notion is based upon the son's having purchased his equal share with his father and uncles by contributing the value of his share in capital goods or cash but retaining his rights as a son nonetheless.

Sons always share equally in the company, even if there is a difference of twenty years in their ages. As soon as the younger is able to do a man's share he will draw his full portion even though he has not been able previously to labor in the maintenance of the company to the same extent that his older brothers have. Although the immature brother does not draw on his share, in terms of yearly gains being set aside for his personal future use, but remains a dependent in his father's household, he is nevertheless considered to own his full share of the company.

The brothers continue to share equally as long as they work together with no consideration being given to the numbers or ages of their children until such a time as they split up or some adjustment is made regarding a disproportionate expenditure of labor in one of the nuclear families.

In the Straits capital goods and property are inherited only through males so that fishing gear, houses, stages, boats, land, and fishing berths [locations for cod traps] are all handed down only from father to sons. However, exceptions have occurred in rare circumstances. For example, a man in a nearby community had only daughters but raised his grandson after his widowed daughter remarried, and the grandson eventually inherited his maternal grandfather's estate. There is also a case in which a boy's father's sister's husband raised him to be his heir as he had no sons. I could only find one instance where a son-in-law came into work with his sonless father-in-law, and it occurred in St. Anthony, outside the Straits area.

Women may inherit domestic goods, but that is all. I have heard sentiments expressed on the part of a few women that this is unfair, particularly in cases where the family was well off. As there was much cash and capital goods to be inherited in these cases the daughters seemed to stand out as being deprived in contrast to their brothers. In most cases, however, the woman finds herself in about the same economic position after marriage as before as, among most people in the area, there is no great difference in economic level. Her work load, amount of leisure time and luxuries will remain about the same. There are cases where fathers stated to their sons that their sisters were to be taken care of if they were even in need.

If there is any cash to be passed on, it is usually left to the youngest son as it is he who most often remains with the parents after he marries. The old family house, or a new house that the parents, or surviving parent, shares with the youngest son and his family is the one in which the brothers often gather and use more freely than each others. As one man said, "We used to be over to our father's house until late almost every night. He loved to talk to us and hated to see us go."

When a man is too old to fish he usually gives up his share and lives "on the mercy of his sons." They provide for his needs and those of their mother. Men now often take their share until they are 65 years old and start collecting old age pensions. As in rural Ireland (Arensberg, 1937:86) the pension provides a small income divorced from the family enterprise which allows the old people to more easily transmit it into the hands of the next generation.

After a man turns over his share he does not necessarily cease all productive efforts. Although not going out in the boats to fish, he may still engage in the numerous activities that the fisherman has ashore such as splitting and drying the cod, knitting twine, mending nets, etc.

People have heard of rare instances where a man, upon retiring, claims "one half of his hand," that is, one half of the income derived from his share. This would be what he would obtain if he employed a shareman to fish his part and, as will be seen later, is the same arrangement which can be made by a widow in retaining rights over her deceased husband's share.

As each son marries he brings his wife to his father's house to

56

live, and, as soon as he is able, builds a house of his own nearby to move into. The amount of time that he remains with his parents after his marriage varies, but five years would be considered a long time. Couples move out faster now than in the past as houses are built more quickly due to the increase in incomes. Before gasoline marine engines arrived in the Straits some 40 years ago, providing power to small saw mills, housebuilding was a more formidable and lengthy undertaking as all planks had to be sawed by hand.[4]

In most cases the youngest son stays with his parents and looks after them when they are old. This is because as the last son he is living with his parents when his brothers have married and moved out. When he marries he will try and build a new house and if the parents are too old to adequately take care of themselves they will move with him. If they are still able to look after themselves they will wait until they have become more aged to move in with him. They "shift over" to the youngest son's because "the other sons have been weaned longer (living out of the parental home) and are more used to their own ways." Parents and the youngest son and his family are also motivated to move because the old house is "out," and more adequate shelter is necessary.

It is much more convenient for the son to look after his aged parents if they are living with him. If they are not, it means his providing a double lot of firewood, water, and keeping up two houses. The old family house is considered to belong to the youngest son when his parents die, and any cash owned by the father is usually left to him. When parents are living together in the same house with a married son, they all have one household account. While the father has his share they share the expense of it.

In some cases there might be difficulties when parents live with a married son, but this is uncommon. "They live together if they can agree," but their not living together does not mean that they can't. There are cases in which a house will be "split" between the parents and son when the latter does not feel that he will be able to build a house for himself and they do not wish to live together. Here the house is partitioned off into two units under the same roof and separate entrances, kitchens, and stairways are put in. One will not find a widower living with his married daughter because "her husband is the boss" in her house and a conflict of authority would ensue. However, "a proper man wouldn't see his father-in-law out on the road."

Brothers contribute any outside income to their fathers for the use of the crew. Thus, when the company lumber camps were open men would turn their paychecks over to their fathers. If an unmarried man has a steady job nearby and lives at home he may turn over his income to his father and receive spending money along with his room and board.

On the other hand, girls who work do not contribute their income, even if living at home, unless it is necessary for the maintenance of the family. It is felt to be necessary in many cases, but males are always expected to do so. The feeling is that the boys are going to stay and take care of the place and will have a permanent share in it; therefore, they must contribute what they earn to the general fund. The girls, in contrast, will marry and leave and consequently have no permanent share in the establishment and thus are not expected to contribute towards it with their outside incomes unless necessary. The daughters of the family do, of course, work hard "at the fish" when they are at home. If a woman does not marry and stays on to help keep up the establishment she may be felt informally to hold some part in the company in some instances widows have had sharemen come in to fish the berths and the gear inherited by their husbands which would eventually be inherited by their sons.

If a man dies leaving no sons big enough to work his share, his brothers see that his wife and children are not in want. Occasionally they merely stay on, living and working with the crew while being supported, but it is preferred that the widow either draw on one-half of the husband's share or take his full share and get a shareman to work it for her. If the widow does not agree to any such arrangements, she is entitled either to all or one-half (informants differ) of the gear making up her husband's share, and she can sell this to her brothers-in-law or to anyone she pleases. Moreover, there were in the past more cases of orphaned children being sent to the orphanage run by the International Grenfell Association in St. Anthony. Now with more welfare funds available, however, I am told that it is not as common.

The lack of uniformity of practice with regard to widows and orphans, like the variations in the case of aged parents, reflects the fact that such decisions are "run by people's opinion." That is, they are not narrowly defined by community sanction or traditional usage, but an accommodation is made on the basis of desires and particular needs of the parties involved.

If the widow sells her deceased husband's share, then it cannot be claimed by her sons, but if she does not, they inherit it whether she draws on it or is merely supported. Whether she takes over the full share and gets a shareman, or takes over only one-half of the share and does not, her proportion of earnings is the same. The implicit principle is that, without someone to put in a man's work in a share, those drawing on it are being supported by the labor of others. Thus, the labor must be provided either by a shareman or by the crew members who receive half "the hand" to divide among themselves for their efforts.

This principle is also involved when a retiring skipper retains half his "hand," and in those cases in which boys whose fathers died before they were grown inherit only the same share of the company as their paternal male cousins rather than their father's full share. It is thought best that orphaned sons inherit their father's full share in the crew regardless of their number relative to the number of their paternal male cousins. Thus, if a man were to leave only one son when he died, that son should inherit his father's full share when he grew up. A situation might accordingly arise in which an orphaned only son would inherit one full share in a crew upon gaining maturity (that of his father) whereas the other share (if he had but one paternal uncle) would be shared by both his paternal uncle and the latter's sons.[5]

An orphaned boy will, accordingly, sometimes share equally with his cousins in the crew rather than automatically taking over his father's entire share. Where this has occurred there were people who felt it was not right. The rationale for such a practice is that the orphan's share was being worked for him and the establishment was being maintained without his aid when he was a dependent, thus reducing his claim.

A widow with grown sons may also be willed a share by her husband to formally provide for herself and her immature sons. Before he died, one man willed a share to his wife and a share each to his four sons. Two of the sons were grown and had their own homes. The other two lived with their mother; one was nineteen and the other was small. She had a shareman to work her part, and in that way her interest and that of the small boy were looked after until he grew up.

Only one instance could be recalled of a woman returning to her natal family when her husband died. In that case the woman's father was a widower and she may have taken over the household duties. The son that she brought with her is now grown and is working with her father's sons and may have an equal share with them.

The "share" then is the mark of permanent male membership in the patrilocal establishment, and is obtained through inheritance and maintained through participation. However, widows sometimes own their part of the concern. Wives are intimately associated with their husbands' participation in the operation, contribute their energies to the crew, as well as to their own households—and are expected to do so permanently —but have no separate share. Similarly, daughters have no share, but they will become permanently associated with the crews of their future husbands and participate in their shares.

There are few exceptions to patrilocal residence. It is considered the normal practice, and the man who does not adhere to it may feel that his real home is his natal settlement, even after long years in his wife's community. Men who have "married in" are sometimes referred to behind their backs by their wives' surnames.[6] This is similar to how in the United States husbands of famous female film stars or celebrities are sometimes jestingly referred to, and the meaning is the same: their prestige is lessened because of their seeming dependence upon their wives or their wives' groups.

Patrilocality is related to women not inheriting capital goods and of a man's economic security lying only with his natal family. The way it is phrased locally is,

> How can a man go to his wife's place when she
> doesn't have anything? And everything that a man
> has is at his home and is a part of what his brothers
> and father have.

The implication when a man marries into his wife's community is that he hadn't enough substance, in capital goods or personality, not to have to rely upon her or her people. There are, however, men who have married in with their own "fit outs" of gear and who are in no way considered in this light. This is also the case when men who have come in from the outside to teach school marry locally.

Along with this we find that the economic situation that women

fiud themselves in after marriage depends much less upon their parents'
standing than in societies in which there is a dowry. The dowry tends
to put a girl in with people of her own or higher economic standing.
Without it, and without arranged marriages, which do not occur in the
Straits, the woman's future position is much more the result of the
chance of individual mate selection. In some cases there may be marked
differences in income between brothers-in-law despite the fact that
economic level is fairly even among people in the area. This does not
mean that relative economic standing is of no consequence in mate
selection. In fact the wealthier families tend to have the most highly
educated girls who often marry professionals or richer men from outside
the community.

Women adapt very well into their new homes after marriage. There
is little, if any, conflict between daughters-in-law and their mothers-in-
law. The chances are that a woman will not be living permanently with
her mother-in-law as it is desirable for each man, other than the youngest
son, to have an independent household. However, a woman can usually look
forward to having a daughter-in-law living permanently with her.

> When a woman marries and moves in with her
> husband's family, she tries to get along the best
> she can. Their ways are a little different than
> yours, and there are things that bother you, but
> you don't show it. You know that one day you will
> have your own house.

Even the wife of the youngest son can look forward to being the
boss in her own home because when her husband builds a new home it is
"hers," even when her mother-in-law moves in with her. By this time much
of the harmony between them is the result of the mother-in-law giving up
most of the management of the daily routine and taking on a less strenuous
regimen. The daughter-in-law becomes more and more responsible for the
cooking, care of children, milking and helping "at the fish" as time goes
by, leaving to the mother-in-law such tasks as mending, assisting with
the cooking, and general dispenser of love and affection to her grandchildre

Prior to this, however, while living in the original home the
mother-in-law is "the head of the women," both in terms of the operation
of her household and in the female labor involved in fish processing.
Within the household the mother-in-law plans the menu and directs the
labor. She will probably take turns cooking with her daughter-in-law,

as two cooking together would get in each other's way. Often the
arrangement is that the woman not cooking does the cleaning, but this
is considered the easier job. Cooking involves seeing that the wood
and water are in and the fire going. The amount of work done by a
daughter-in-law varies from none to one-half, but a typical situation
would be the mother cooking two weeks for the daughter-in-law's one,
and the latter washing only her own and her husband's clothes.

The fact that she does less work in the home than her husband's
mother, probably not much more than she did in her parents' home,
probably facilitates her adjustment. In fact, she is treated by her
mother-in-law as a daughter and should "act just like she would in her
own home." One woman said that her mother-in-law would feel just as
bad if she died as she would if one of her own daughters died. They
are less likely to get along if the daughter-in-law "doesn't know how
to do anything"--increasingly the situation these days--and is not willing
to learn.

After a woman marries she finds herself more and more involved
with her husband's people and less and less with her own. "When a
woman is married, she leaves her own family and joins her husband's
family." This is the case whether she is from the same settlement as
her husband or comes in from the outside. At first there is much
visiting of her natal family but this decreased over time. A woman
finds herself increasingly involved with her affines, both in her
participation in mutual tasks, such as helping together at the fish,
and in terms of economic interest. She realizes more and more that what
she owns is also owned by her sisters-in-law and other affines.

The influence of the extended family can be seen in the pattern
of land tenure and the expansion of settlement in Savage Cove. Land can
be inherited, purchased, or obtained by clearing a hitherto unused area.
With the exception of one unused strip, there is no granted land in
Savage Cove. Granted land is land that has been surveyed, deeded, and
is legally owned. Despite the fact that land is not granted, it is
still inherited and sometimes purchased, and the rights of the owners are
in all ways locally respected. People assert that if their claim on the
land was ever contested, they would have first choice in having it granted.

Areas owned consist of land upon which the house stands and which surrounds the house; gardens, which are usually upon the latter; meadows, which are often adjacent to the house; and fishing berths which are close offshore.

When a man's boys grow up and marry they tend to build houses on land adjacent to his. This necessitates clearing the land if it has not already been cleared for meadow. As land is plentiful, there is usually no problem in finding a vacant area upon which a house can be built nearby. Along with the new house there will be a new garden and outbuildings. However, the structures utilized in fishing will probably not be added to as there has been no change in the crew structure. On the north side of the cove the original settlers settled some distance apart and the areas around the original homesites have now been occupied by their agnatic descendants, people generally living on land and using meadows adjacent to those of the original settlers. The situation on the south side is somewhat different for two reasons. First, because the people living on that side tended to build houses in various places and also moved them (the houses). Secondly, since the development of Charl't'on, some who moved there have left their old establishments on the southside. They still own the old house sites and the old meadows.

Land is only owned up to thirty feet of the shoreline. Thus, anyone can build wharves and stages anywhere, as long as they do not interfere with ones already established. Here the land is not owned, but the structures are inherited.

The youngest son thus inherits the father's homestead with his brothers making their homes nearby by either clearing new land or utilizing meadow land already cleared and claimed by the father. Land has rarely been bought and sold, but there are two instances of it. In both cases it was purchased from members of the Hodge family that has now left the community. In one case a widow was leaving and the land was purchased by another resident of the north side, as much to aid her as anything, as he did not need the land. He then sold it later to a man from the south side who moved over to the north side. In the other case three brothers from the north side bought property belonging to another family of the same group who had moved away. This illustrates the permanency of land claims. If it were merely a matter of occupancy and use there would have been no reason for money to be exchanged in the latter cases. However, if land has not been used or occupied for a long period of time people begin to say that it doesn't really belong to anyone even though it is still claimed by the descendants of the previous owners.

In the Straits, then, the patrilocal extended family is a named social and economic corporation in which the male members have shares, split the profits and the work equally. Wives' positions are derivative in the sense that they partake in their husbands' shares and come to identify themselves with their stake, both socially and economically in the joint venture, although widowed women are sometimes considered to have their husbands' parts. Daughters have no share; however, if women do not marry but stay in the group to work there may be some feeling that they own their part of the outfit in an undefined way, but they still have no formal share. Boys, on the other hand, have a potential share, and this is recognized, now that there is more cash and more danger of their not staying with the crew, by their sometimes receiving a certain amount in cash for their part of the year's fishing.

This corporation normally extends over three generations, although it sometimes extends over four. In the latter case two groups of brothers who are first cousins to each other will continue to cooperate.

This corporation maintains joint ownership of capital goods and maintains a regular system of patrilineal inheritance. In a sense there is no inheritance of capital goods, but merely a reallocation of shares. The father, unless he dies prematurely, becomes an equal shareholder with his sons before his death and so what was originally only his property (before it was added to by his sons' efforts) is already held in common with his sons. What they do in effect is jointly take over what had been his share when alive to divide it when they separate. This was born out by a discussion between two men as to whether or not a son who had taken his share of the gear and left the family was entitled to his part of his father's share after his father died.

This grouping does not maintain a common residence, but adult married sons tend to live next to their parents although some live in other parts of the community. Authority is patriarchal with men being clearly dominant over women and the father, or in his stead the older brother being the leader.

Company Fission

From the point of view of structure the critical linkage in the
extended family is the relationship between brothers. This is so for
three reasons: first, it provides the point of fission and fragmentation
of the group as well as the essential nexus of co-operation; secondly,
local sentiment stresses this connection to the detriment of the connection
between generations, thus mitigating against establishment of a descent
group; and thirdly, the same end is furthered by the fact that only those
in the first and second generations have actual shares in the enterprise.

Where extended families endure for three generations (the males
comprising the founder, his adult sons, and their pre-adult sons) one finds
a split in every generation. A crew of brothers ideally does not separate
after their father dies but does so when the brothers' sons become mature.
Then each brother becomes the skipper of his own crew which is composed
of himself and his sons as shareholders. This may be diagrammed as
follows (the circles include only the adult males within crews):

CHART II

The Three Generation Extended Family

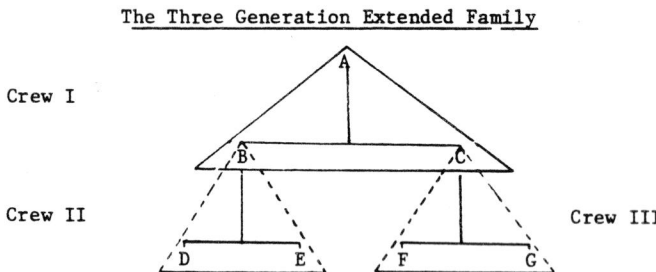

Crew I

Crew II

Crew III

While Crew I exists it is composed of A, B, and C as shareholders
but D, E, and F, G are dependents having only potential shares in Crews
II and III respectively. Before Crew I splits up the founder, A, will
have died and his share will have been absorbed by his sons, B and C.
They will split when their sons become mature. When this occurs each will
become a founder of a new crew and his sons will become partners with him.
Therefore, each man as an adult is a member of two crews, the one in which
he has an equal share as a brother and the one he founds as a father. He
cedes from his brothers in the former, but remains with sons who in turn
will cede from their brothers to head their own crews.

Linkage between brothers, aside from being the point of fragmentation, is also the essential connection in terms of continuing
co-operation within the group as the sons carry on and absorb their
father's part. The father has the same share as his sons and it is
the sons who provide the bulk of the labor of the crew.

The same situation prevails in the once more prevalent and
presumably older, four-generation family, diagrammed as follows:

CHART III

The Four Generation Extended Family

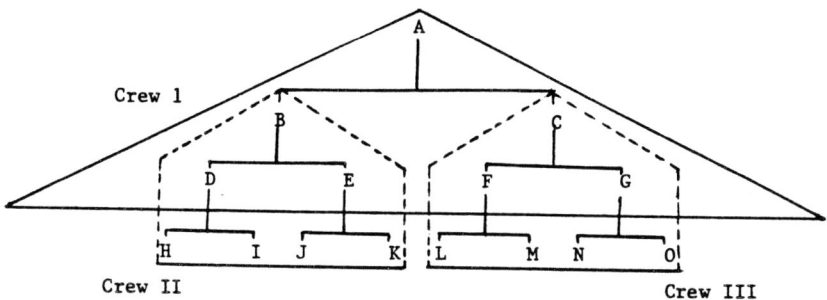

The four-generation extended family is a result of brothers
(B and C) not separating, but continuing together after their boys
become adult. Their sons, then, as adults remain in the group to make
up the third generation even though they have no shares. The death of
the founder of the crew, (A) does not disturb the unity of the group
nor does the coming to maturity of the founder's grandsons (D, E, F,
and G), but the death of one of the brothers (B and C) usually causes
the split.

So while Crew I exists, it is composed of A, B, C, D, E, F, and
G. Only A, B, and C hold shares in the enterprise with D and E, and F
and G, as fully participating adults having only potential shares in the
crews that their fathers will someday head. The fourth generation, H
through O, are dependent children. Crew I continues on after A dies
with B and C as the only shareholders. The separation again is between
brothers B and C, but only late in their lives or between one brother
and his sons and the sons of the other brother after the latter's demise.
After the split D and E join B as shareholders in Crew II if B is living,

if not, the eldest of D and E becomes skipper. Similarly, F and G join
C as shareholders in Crew III if C is living, if not, the eldest brother
becomes skipper. Note that D, E, F and G had no shares in Crew I even
though they were adult participating members of Crew I; H, I, J and K
have no shares in Crew II and L, M, N, and O have no shares in Crew III
even though they are adult participating members of these crews.

The essential nexus of co-operation is still brothers D and E,
and F and G carry on together after their father has died, and H and I,
J and K, L and M, and N and O will make up the nexuses of future crews.

If we were to utilize Radcliffe-Brown's principles of the unity
of the sibling group and of the unity of the lineage (Radcliffe-Brown,
1952) as sentiments about groupings rather than structural principles,
we should be able to say that in the Straits the emphasis is on the
sibling group rather than on the lineage.[7] That is, it is of consequence
whether or not brothers stay together: a positive value is placed upon
such behavior. It is expected as part of continuing social life. On
the other hand, there is no feeling that a specific agnatic unit should
continue through time via upcoming generations. It is not held important
that cousins remain working together within an unfragmented group, but
it is the ideal that brothers work together all their lives. This
would usually produce a group in which adult cousins worked together,
but this is merely a result of their fathers' continued co-operation, and
is not conceived as an ideal feature in itself.

Such values are commensurate with the disappearance of extended
families in which brothers held together all their adult lives. Without
a sentiment emphasizing the maintenance of a descent group, prolonged
association would yield to such influences as an increased amount of
cash in the economy and alternate forms of employment.

The increase in cash in the area in recent years has undoubtedly
influenced the development of both family accounts and the three-generation
family. With little or no cash there would be no conspicuous difference
in distribution among the nuclear families of a crew. The head of each
nuclear family had to ask the skipper for anything not ordinarily obtained
for the extended family as a whole, but since there was little or no cash
for such items there would be little danger of disproportionate distribution.
Even when cash was earned there would be little problem because as "times

were hard" in the past it would take all that one could earn to provide the more essentials of food, clothing, and shelter. However, with an increase of cash the problem of distribution develops. With a surplus beyond meager subsistance to be divided among the nuclear families inequalities would soon develop if the division is entirely dependent upon periodic and personal solicitation of the skipper. Hence, an equal division of funds in terms of family accounts helps insure against discord caused by actual or fancied unequal distribution. All shareholders get equal parts despite any variation in the number of their children.

Similarly, the change from a four- to a three-generation family is undoubtedly related to an increase in cash. Division is equal among brothers (the second generation), but as they will probably have unequal numbers of boys (the third generation), who only have a part in their father's share, it would be difficult for the four-generation family to continue. If there were no cash, on the other hand, the matter of unequal distribution in the third generation would not arise as there would be no surplus whose division would be a problem. As an illustration let us present a hypothetical crew founded by A, now deceased, that includes his two sons, B and C. B has one son, E, and C has two sons F and G. The only shares are those of B and C as A is dead. B and C have family accounts and an unequal number of sons. As the income of the group is divided equally between B and C the disparity between the income of E and the income of one of C's sons would become evident if they remained in the crew after setting up their own nuclear families. The only way in which each son can get an even share of the income of his crew is by splitting into two groups (that of B and E, and that of C, F, and G): thus, eliminating both the permanent association of brothers in a crew and the possibility of the extended family lasting four generations.

CREW IV

Inheritance Example

Therefore, an accommodation on one level, that of establishing family accounts to insure equality of distribution among shareholders, makes for the dropping of one generation from the extended family as it, in most instances, would lead to an automatic inequality in the third generation.

We have been speaking of a crew almost as if it contained only adult male members, but, of course, it includes wives and children. Wives and children are not only in the extended family group but also work at the fish and so may also be considered a part of the work crew. Shares in a crew are held only by the founder and his sons, however, so that in a four-generation extended family one finds adult males (grandsons of the founder) who are crew members but have no shares.

Nuclear Families as Domestic Groups

The houses of the settlements line the shores of the coves and, except for many of the new bungalow style homes now being built, are generally oriented towards the water, their fronts facing the sea.[8] The typical house is a wooden, frame structure of two stories. It is square in ground plan with a low pitched roof rising from the four walls to a small, central, flat square through which the chimney rises. The ground floor contains a kitchen, a sitting room, and a dining room. The front door usually leads into the sitting room and is almost never used, the back door being the usual means of entrance and exit. The front door is opened on warm days for ventilation or used if the back door becomes snowed in during the winter. It opens onto a platform called the bridge, seemingly comparable in position to the similarly named structure on a ship.

The sitting room is little used, as the kitchen is the social center of the house. There will be a chesterfield set and a set of coffee and end tables in the sitting room if the family is moderately well off. If not, there may be only a chesterfield or a few straight chairs. The walls of the sitting room are typically decorated with religious pictures, particularly ones of Christ and the Last Supper, as well as mottoes expressing religious and familial sentiments and family photographs. Though not strictly reserved for formal use it tends to be used on formal occasions such as weddings and funerals and infrequently otherwise. In many houses this room contains the stairway

to the second floor, and so is more often used as a passageway than
as a sitting room.

The upstairs is used solely for sleeping quarters, and the dining
room tends to be used only at mealtimes although some families tend to
linger there and talk after meals. The kitchen is where the members
of the family normally spend time together, talking, sewing, napping,
playing, studying. It is that part of the house which articulates the
household with the rest of the community as members of other households
come and go freely in the kitchen, but do not usually enter the rest
of the house. In this sense it is semi-public, whereas the rest of the
house is reserved for the privacy of the occupants.

In the kitchen are to be found a stove, a kitchen table and chairs,
a settle [day bed] or wooden bench, and sometimes a sink. The stove
is a wood range in which sometimes a little coal is burned in the winter.
Wood is preferred as coal is expensive ($30.00 a ton), dirty to handle
and sooty to burn. However, it lasts longer and a little added to a
wood fire keeps it going well. Wood is chopped by the men rather than
purchased, burns clean and burns hotter than coal. The fire is started
with splits [kindling] and kerosene in the morning and is kept going
during the day, at least during the winter time. In the past, men
would make shavings with a two-handled drawing knife with which to start
the fire, thus saving the expense of kerosene. The fire is kept up with
junks of wood from the woodbox near the stove. These are brought in by
the children or the wife from the stack on the porch which in turn comes
from the wood-pile outdoors which consists of long sticks stacked up in
tipi fashion to form a tall cone.[9]

The stove is placed so that its back is to the inside kitchen
wall, and in many houses its pipe goes through the upstairs hall to give
off heat on the second floor. Quite often a chair is to be found on the
right hand side of the stove near the fire box and is the favorite
haunt of people coming in from the cold. Visitors come indoors out of
freezing weather and bask in the heat of the stove without removing any
garments only to get up and go directly out into the cold. Children
sometimes hide behind the stove when strangers come in and also like
to huddle on the chair by the firebox. Wet mitts and socks are hung
to dry upon a rod behind the stove or sometimes put into the warming
ovens. The kettle is usually on.

That the kitchen serves as a common room is related to material matters. It is the warmest room in the house during the long, cold winters, particularly in the homes of those with less income. Here the kitchen stove may be the only source of warmth in the house, there being no supplementary oil or coal stove in the sitting room. The scarcity of light sources also has its influence. Except for the houses that have only in recent years acquired electric lights powered by portable generators, lighting is by kerosene lamps, and it is much easier for many to gather around one lamp than to have several lamps burning simultaneously in various rooms.

However, the communality of the kitchen reflects the intimacy, "openness," and lack of desire for privacy which characterizes the area: people relish company and visiting, men sit close together and sometimes sprawl upon each other when on the settle, and letters are passed around and read by the entire family.

The kitchen always contains either a settle, or lockers, a bench having a sloping back rest at one end and internal compartments to which access is gained by hinged portions of the seat. These items of furniture reflect the use of the kitchen as a room in which people spend much of their time. The men of the house nap or recline on them, and when visitors come in they may sit along them. Day beds were homemade until recently, as was all furniture. In lieu of springs the homemade day beds had rope lacings. At one time kitchens contained little wooden benches on which children were dressed by the stove in the morning.

A sink and mirror are often found in the kitchen. Here people do their "washing up" or use pitchers and basins upstairs. Children are often washed at the sink in the kitchen before going to bed. There is also another sink in a pantry off the kitchen in which dishes are washed. Hot water for washing comes from the saddle tank in the stove or from the kettle, whence comes the tea water. Some houses have basement wells or pipes running to neighborhood wells. These have pumps in the pantry by the sink or in the porch, but they freeze at some point during the winter, and the family is forced to obtain water in the same manner as those without pumps, by carrying it from a neighborhood well. This is done with a barrel mounted on a carry-all [hand drawn sled] in winter and with a bucket or a covul [a barrel mounted with handles] in the summer.

The porch is a small enclosed room which leads outside from the
kitchen. There may be two porches, one a corner room inside the house
and another adjoining it built onto the house. These provide doors which
separate the kitchen from the outside. To come into the kitchen from
outdoors one must go through the outside door, the porch door--if there
are two porches--and the kitchen door. This provides one or two "airlocks"
between the kitchen and the outside, thus conserving heat, and also serves
to warn the family when someone is entering as traversing this area and
opening and shutting the doors is not done without noise. They are then
prepared to terminate any conversation which would not be suitable for
the ears of the newcomer. The front door, in contrast, opens directly
outside from the sitting room. Most kitchens are built on the east or
southeast corner of the house (depending upon how it is oriented), which
shelters it, the porch and the back door from the prevailing cold northwest
wind. The waterbarrel is often kept in the porch and coats may be hung
on pegs on the walls.

Metal bands or wooden frames are sometimes mounted under kitchen
tables for use in knitting twine [making netting]. The bundle of twine
is placed on the frame which then rotates as the twine is pulled off as
needed. In the past such wooden frames might be suspended from the ceiling.

The family eats in the kitchen if there is no dining room. In the
dining room are to be found a large table, chairs and usually a buffet
for dishes and silverware. There are four meals a day: breakfast, from
8:00 a.m. to 9:00 a.m.; dinner at noon; supper around 5:00 or 6:00; and
a lunch before retiring at night. Some families have an additional lunch
during the day, and a very few have two additional meals. Breakfast was
at one time predominantly fish and brewis [hard bread and fish cooked
together] but it is becoming more and more an eggs-bacon-and-toast meal,
among those who can afford it, except on Sundays when baked beans are
traditional. Dinner is the main meal of the day with meat being served
on Sunday, Tuesday, and Thursday and with fish Monday, Wednesday and
Friday. Split pea soup is a popular Saturday dinner. Suppers consist
of bread, leftovers from dinner, cheese, macaroni, tinned meat, bologna,
potatoes. Everyone has "a cup of tea" or a lunch before going to bed,
and both these terms refer to a fairly substantial meal which is sweeter
than supper although the volume of food is much the same. Children are
usually given bread with jam or molasses fairly informally before going
to bed, but most adults sit down to the table.

ILLUSTRATION I

HOUSE PLANS

TYPICAL HOUSE

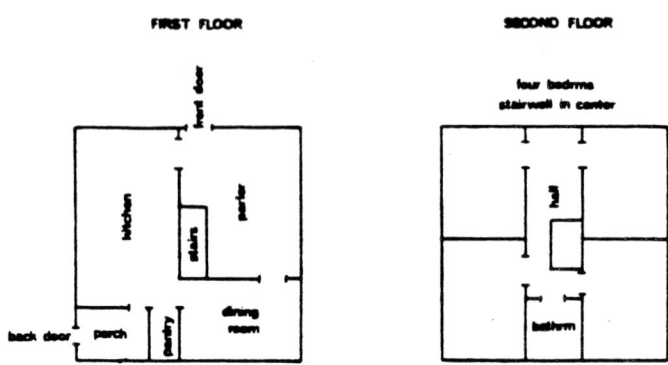

OLDER STYLE HOUSE

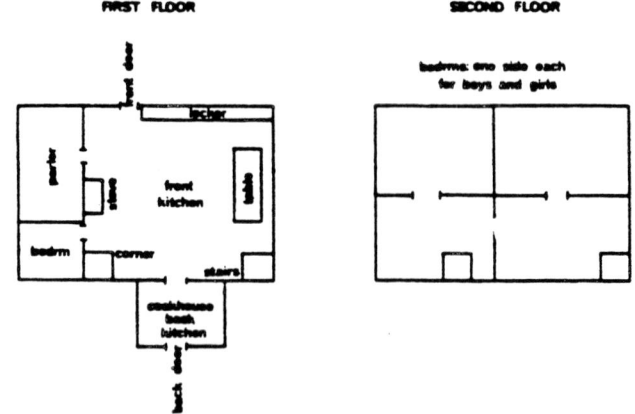

Grace is said before meals, usually by the mother but sometimes by one of the children or the father. The most commonly said is found in the Common Prayer and Hymn Book (1962:735): "For what we are about to receive, may the Lord make us truly thankful; through Jesus Christ our Lord. Amen." Since families are large, there are sometimes more people than can sit around the table and it is necessary to have two sittings. When this is the case the men and boys eat first.

The second floor consists of a central hallway along which there are small bedrooms. There are usually five or six little bedrooms furnished with double beds and dressers. There may be a bathroom in which chamber pots are kept or, if not, there is a chamber pot in each room. Some of the newer houses have closets, but in the older ones clothes are hung flat against the wall on hooks or folded and kept in chests. Chests used to be homemade, contained tills and could be painted to match the color of the room or hall in which they sat. Girls who shipped out [went outside the community to work] might have their own chest.

One room is occupied by the parents, the other rooms by the children. The youngest child shares a bed with his parents until supplanted by a younger sibling or until he is about three years old. As families are large and space is limited, particularly when a shareman, a girl who has shipped out, or a school teacher is living in the house, children may sleep three or four in a bed. People do not like to sleep alone and almost always keep an oil lamp burning as a night light. No one would spend the night in a house by himself, and most men dislike camping in the woods alone at night. This fear of isolation in the dark, somewhat due to the fear of spirits [ghosts], is perhaps, like the threat to the child that the fearful fantasy figure will take him away from family and local society, a reflection of the intimacy that permeates social relations.

The newest houses are bungalows with bedrooms built off a long hallway. They have basements and oil heating, and the living room is more used. There are also older, small single story dwellings, and some of an old style which have two floors, steeply pitched roofs, and exposed ceiling beams.

This older style had two rooms in which food was cooked: the front kitchen and the back kitchen or cook house. The cook house was

a small enclosed porch built onto the rear of the house behind the front
kitchen, which occupied most of the first floor. In the summer the
family would eat in the cook house, and meals would be prepared there
as it was cool. In the winter the food would be cooked and meals
taken in the front kitchen which used to be, and is still sometimes,
referred to as the house. In the winter the cook house was packed with
wood.

The front kitchen occupied most of the ground floor and the front
door opened into it instead of into the parlor. A locker generally ran
along the front kitchen wall between the corner and the front door.
The stairway was generally in the front kitchen and this might be a
circular corner stairway. The parlor and a single bedroom, usually
occupied by the parents comprised the remainder of the ground floor,
and both were small compared to the kitchen. These were built one
behind the other at one side of the house. Often there was a hole cut
in the parlor wall into which was fitted the back of the kitchen stove.
With a mantle piece built above it, for heating purposes. The upstairs
consisted of bedrooms, usually used by the children. In some houses
the upstairs was partitioned into a private section for the boys and
one for the girls, each part having its own stairway.

Some settlements in the Straits had winter communities that were
used for half of the year while others had houses a short distance away
in the woods for winter use. One man suggested that having a cook house
was an accommodation developed with the abandonment of this winter shifting.

Most families have a cow kept in a small wooden barn near the house.
The women do the milking and care for the cows. Milking is done both
morning and night when necessary or only at night if the cow is not giving
much milk. In late spring after the dogs are barred in [penned up] the
cows are loose to graze at night and wander a fair distance from home.
The women must find them and drive them home and so morning milking may
be time consuming. Each family usually has a calf which is killed in
the winter when the weather has become sufficiently cold to facilitate
storage. The few bulls in the area wander loose. No one is afraid of
them and young children even chase them.

Meadows, often to be found near houses, were at one time fenced
off so that the hay could grow undisturbed for winter use. Now more

hay is purchased and cows graze where they will. Hay is also cut in
meadows "in the country," and some men go to St. Anthony, where no cows
are kept, to cut the hay from people's yards. In the past some in other
communities went across to the Labrador to cut hay.

There is a garden near the house. Most families have their own,
but sometimes married brothers may share in one. There are picket fences
around the gardens, which usually being not too firmly set in the ground,
are sometimes knocked down by raiding cows and horses. The gardens are
put in by the women with the help of the children in the late spring,
before fishing starts. The chief produce is potatoes, turnips, cabbage,
carrots, and beets which are stored in turf-covered cellars.

The settlers in northern Newfoundland and Labrador took over the
entire Eskimo dog traction complex including the kamotik [sled], dog
whip, and moccasins [little bags, here of canvas, to cover and protect
the dogs' feet]. Most families no longer have dog teams, as they have
acquired snowmobiles and trucks to supplant them. However, the structures
which went with keeping dogs still stand near many houses. These are
the pound, the scaffold, and the vate. The pound is a square palisade
of upright poles in which the dogs are shut during the summer and fall.
They have no openings as the dogs are lowered in in the spring and
hauled out when the snow begins. In some communities in the past the
dogs would be let out once a day to drink brook water and eat fish scraps
around the stages. They returned to the pounds at the cry of "house in."
Sometimes a small roofed shed is attached to the pound to offer more
shelter. The scaffold is a platform the height of the palisade upon
which meat and fish are kept to be thrown down into the pound at feeding
time, about five o'clock. The vate is a small shed with a tiny door in
which salt fish is put away for the dogs' later use.

The house is more the woman's world than the man's. She is there
most of the time in all seasons, being absent longest in the late summer
and autumn when helping with the fish. Then, she and the other women of
the crew go down to the stages and help split and salt and spread the
fish to dry in the sun. Such absence poses some problems in household
management during this period, but the women are not gone so long that
they cannot keep the house and meals in minimal order. Infants may be
watched by older siblings, or in their absence left tucked securely in
cradles by themselves.

Women, of course, leave the house to visit and shop and attend church and C.E.W.A. meetings, and go to times and sometimes restaurants, but by and large their primary focus is the home, and domestic affairs are entirely in their hands.

Men, on the other hand, use the home more as a base camp from which they go forth to either the sea or the woods, as the exigencies of making a living demand. During the first part of the fishing season the men go out to their offshore traps twice a day, or perhaps go off for a few hours trawling or jigging. However, at the end of the season they follow the fish across to the Labrador side, and there they stay in tilts [small shacks] and tents for a few weeks. Before the lumber camps closed down most would be off working in the woods during the fall. In both cases they return on Sundays, if possible. Men leave to spend time in the woods hunting and sometimes these trips are of long duration.

Men's coming and going is an informal affair. Plans are usually not laid far in advance regarding times of departure and women are not consulted regarding them. The men leave when they feel fitting, often upon very short notice, and the women arrange their affairs to meet the men's schedule. A woman does not know exactly when her men will return, but when they do, no matter what time of day or night, she sees that they are fed and properly attended to. Often one man out of a crew remains behind when the men are over on the Labrador or in the country to look after the heavier chores such as keeping up the wood supply.

The women worry about the men when they are away, particularly when they are off fishing on the Labrador or out on the ice after seals, and anxiously seek news of their men from those who have returned. Grandmothers will say that they have had "a life of worry." Once, during a sealing season when seals were scarce a man remarked jokingly that there must be witches keeping them off. His mother said in reply, "If you hear about anybody doing that, it's me." She would rather the seals not appear than the men endure the dangers of the pursuit.

Just as the men come and go from the community while the women stay, so men's movements are much more free about the community than women's as women's duties require their more constant attendance upon the home. The men do more visiting in the evenings, and on the north

side of the settlement some are usually found congregated in one of the
houses which serves as an informal meeting place for the men of that
half of the community. Here they chat and discuss the events of the day.
It is strictly a man's meeting with the women of the house the only women
present. Men also have a greater chance to get about during the day as
their work activities mostly lie outside of the home and as the work
pattern is one of cigarette breaks and conversation punctuating hard
work, there is ample time for socializing.

Men and women do not go about together much after marriage. Courting
couples may go to times together, but married men and women may arrive
separately. Married couples arrive at church together and go to concerts
together and sometimes visit together, but that is all. Just recently
card parties involving both sexes have begun, but traditionally, only the
men would play. Some younger married women are beginning to feel that
their husbands should stay home occasionally to help with the children
and allow them more freedom to go out.

Women do not smoke, although some of the younger women have now
started, nor drink, except for a little wine at Christmas. These taboos
are symbolic of the male-female status differential. To partake in such
male prerogatives would be "brazen" and imply assertiveness. Men have
said that they did not feel like a man until they started smoking.

The family is patriarchal. Decisions pertaining to family activities
are ultimately those of the father, and the plans of a group of brothers
working together under their father are finalized by him. In the house
the woman gets a drink for her husband from the water barrel or food on
his demand. It is the nature of the tone of the communication that
indicates the nature of the relationship. The man tells his wife to do
whatever it is that he wants in a manner of fact way—neither a command
nor a request—and she complies. There is no question as to the man's
authority nor to the woman's subordination.

Women will say that "it is best when the wife does what the
husband wants," and that "a good woman here is one who is obedient and
doesn't try and tell the man what to do—at least the men would say
that." Women know that in order to get along this is the best way to
act. There are, of course, some couples who do not get along, and while
they do not fight openly, they are "nasty" to one another.

Along with the woman's position goes a great deal of security.

Her role and authority in the home is defined, there is no divorce, and very little disharmony among married couples. There is no question about the worth or necessity of women in the home.

As mentioned previously women are expected to take their husbands' religion if they marry a man of a different faith. This is true even in the few cases where Roman Catholic women have married men of other faiths; however, men of other faiths say, "it is hard to get" Catholic girls. It is said that in this way the family is not weakened by disunity and disagreement and "the children know what they are." However, fundamentalists, now making converts in the area, are viewed with concern as they encourage their members to convert those in their families, and this is said to lead to conflict. There are instances of marriages of mixed religion between individuals of the three established religions in the area in which the woman refused to take her husband's religion and both took up fundamentalism as a compromise. A man who once lived in the community had daughters who married men of other faiths and sons who became fundamentalists. Illustrating the patrilineal sentiments involved, he sadly said that he would have expected his daughters to make the change under the circumstances, but he never thought his sons would. Thus one can see that family solidarity and harmony are thought to be related to male authority in these matters, especially as a bride will be residing with a number of her husband's agnates after marriage.

The Rites of Passage as Family Rituals

The rights of passage are, basically, family rituals. In the past mothers were concerned with having names for their children before they were born, for if the infants died unnamed and unbaptized they could not be buried in the sanctified burying ground. Little graves would sometimes be dug near the graveyard to accommodate such deaths and to forestall such a situation the nurses at the Grenfell Nursing Station would sometimes perform an emergency service over the infant if it was felt that it might not live. Today, with the lower rate of infant mortality some mothers do not decide upon a name until well after the child's birth. There was, until recently, much use of midwives, but their employment has been falling off since the nursing station was established in the 1930s. Now, most women deliver at the Station.

Baptism involves the selection of godparents. This is done informally with either friends or any relatives taking the parts. Not much is made of god parenthood. In response to questions about the relationship between godparent and godchild I have heard adults say that godparents should actively take up the responsibility of the child's religious training, but they, for the most part, do not do this. However, the establishment of any serious band of obligation between godparent and child as happens in Latin America, would not be in keeping with local egalitarian and competitive society.

Confirmation occurs in late childhood during the visit of the bishop or archbishop which takes place every other year. An arch of evergreen bows is constructed in front of the church to honor his visit.

Prior to weddings the banns are published three times. The bride's boys and the bride's girls do the work involved in the wedding tea [reception] as well as acting as ushers and bridesmaids at the ceremony. If there is to be no reception then there may be only two of each: "Just someone to witness the marriage." The best bride's girl and the best bride's boy sign the marriage certificate as witnesses. The maximum is about five for a big wedding and if it is thought that there were more than appropriate it will be commented that "there were bride's girls enough!" The bride's boys are chosen by the groom, usually from among his friends and brothers while the bride's girls are selected by the bride from among her sisters and friends.

The father-giver, the man who gives the bride away, may or may not be the bride's father. If the father does not perform the bride may choose any man, but usually this is an uncle or older brother. Although I have heard that in such cases the father, "just wouldn't like the idea of giving away his daughter," he probably disapproves. "In some cases the daughters don't even ask their father, you know they got a feelin' how they [their father] feels towards it."

In the last few years the order of procession during the marriage ceremony has changed in Savage Cove. In the past the bride came first with the father-giver, and after them came the groom and the best bride's girl. At the chancel the father-giver stepped back and the groom stepped up to the bride. The bride's girls stood to the left of the aisle along the chancel and the bride's boys to the right. Now, the groom goes to the chancel by himself and waits and then the father-giver and the bride come up and the bride stands by the groom. The change probably represents the adoption of the urban standard practice. As the bride and groom emerge from the church men fire off guns.

In the past there would be two teas, one at the bride's parents' home on the day of the wedding and one at the groom's parents' home on the next day. If the groom was from a different settlement the wedding party would journey there on the second day. The bride and groom would put on their wedding clothes in either case on the second day and guns would be fired as they started off. Today there is but one reception and it is at the bride's home or in the school house. The groom and his family often contribute to the expense and preparation of the tea.

If the tea is held in a house the newly married couple will be seated in one of the rooms and the guests will go in and "wish them much joy" and get a bride knot [ribbon]. "Special people," such as the brothers and sisters and uncles and aunts may also wear a rose.

The first "table" [sitting] of the tea includes the minister, the bride and groom, their parents and usually older people and special guests. There is no special second table or other tables--whoever is present is served until the food is all gone.[10]

Dancing follows the tea with the bride and groom being involved in the first dance together with the bride's boys and girls and the father-giver. Haste to the Wedding was in the past the opening tune.

In the early days couples were sometimes married by laymen until the minister came around to perform the service. An enclosure in the mission records (M.S.B.I.) dated October 3rd, 1876, at L'anse au Loup:[11]

> This is to certify that,
>   We, William Buckle and Selina Picco . . .
> are about to be married by Mr. W. How [a licensed
> Lay Reader] on the premises of Messrs. Watson &
> Short do hereby promise that we will present
> ourselves to the first clergyman who shall visit
> our shores to receive the blessing of the Church
> on our marriage and we do also promise to pay him
> at that time the customary fee--
>
>   Signed William Buckle
>   Selina + Picco
>   her mark
>
>   Witness Nathan + Northoren
>   his mark

After death the deceased lies in his own home until the burial which is always on the third day, that is, on the second day after the day of the death. If a person did not die at home he would be carried back to his own house so that he might lie there until the burying. The house in which the corpse lies is called the dead house, and this term is also extended to the mortuaries that exist in towns.

The "box" is not made ahead of time in anticipation of a death. The corpse is measured and a coffin is made to fit him. No particular person makes the coffin, just "anybody who can do a bit of carpentry." The coffin is "cased" with purple cloth and fitted with handles. A poor family will have only a plain box with a piece of rope through either end for lowering.

The corpse is washed and dressed in a new suit. In the past women used to cut winding sheets in a diamond shaped pattern, but not lace, much like the material in lace curtains, is used. Those who attend the corpse in this fashion are asked to by someone in the family and no one of the family participates.

A wake is held on the two nights before the burial. Many people will come during the early part of the night, but at least one person who is outside the family must be there through the night to keep the fire in. Hymns are sung.

On the day of the funeral people assemble at the house of the deceased. Those who "own the corpse" send for the minister, and he usually arrives in the late morning. People assemble early, perhaps beginning to arrive at 9:30. It is best to go early as one knows the service will begin sometime before noon, but not exactly when. No one is explicitly invited to attend--all who wish may do so.

Before the service small groups stand talking and waiting outside the house and people stand and sit inside the house, viewing the corpse and mournfully waiting.

During this time the overbearers and the underbearers are picked out. The underbearers are six men who carry the coffin. The overbearers or topbearers, are an equal number who hold the pall, a large white sheet upon which a black cross has been sewn, over the coffin and the underbearers when the latter carry the coffin.

The night before the funeral someone will write down the list of mourners. Anyone can do the writing but someone in the family will tell them who to put down. This is a list of relatives who will line up behind the coffin to march when their names are called.

After the minister arrives the next morning and "prays over the corpse" there is a general rush to view the body before the coffin is shut. The underbearers then carry the coffin out of the house and place it on the waiting komatik. As they do so the overbearers hold the pall over the coffin and their heads. The coffin is then lashed to the komatik with the pall covering it.

Next, "reading the mourners" takes place. As the coffin rests on the komatik the list prepared the previous night is read, and as their names are called the mourners line up in two's behind the coffin. The komatik is pulled by the underbearers and the funeral procession starts off to the church with the official mourners following directly behind the coffin and everyone else coming behind.

Before the coming of the road the komatik was used both summer and winter, but now the entire journey is usually made by truck except for the distance between the road and the graveyard where the komatik is still used at least in the winter.

Upon arriving at the church the coffin is carried in in the same manner as it left the dead house, by the underbearers while the over-bearers held the pall over it and them. It leaves the church in the same manner and is taken from the komatik into the graveyard in the same fashion.

The service is read in the church by the minister, or in his absence a teacher. Canon Richards' eulogies were much appreciated as since he had served in the area for such a long period he was able to give a full life history of many of those he buried.

At the grave side the service proceeds and hymns are sung. Afterwards everyone files away while a few men fill the grave. The grave itself is adjacent to those of other members of the same family, either in the same row or in an adjacent row. People who have left a community to live permanently elsewhere sometimes are brought back to be buried in their natal settlement if they have none of their family buried at their new place of residence.

The grave markers are of stone, many carrying the insignia of the Orange Lodge, but there are still a few of wood to be found, their lettering now effaced by the elements. The graves are decorated in some instances by an outline of stones or sea shells. Often they are outlined by a wooden or cement frame in the shape of a coffin. Many families take care to leave real or artificial flowers on the graves frequently. The graveyards are surrounded by white wooden fences whose posts are sometimes mounted with ornamentally cut knobs.

The period of mourning is ideally an entire year, but is rarely kept that long today. During this period the window blinds were kept down night and day, a band of black crepe was worn around a sleeve and a band of black around the cap, and mourners would not engage in any entertainments.

The order in which the mourners are called and march is as follows:

        The surviving spouse
        The children of the deceased
        The spouses of the above
        The parents of the deceased
        The grandparents of the deceased
        The brothers and sisters of the deceased
        The spouses of the above
        The grandchildren of the deceased

The children and the siblings of the deceased walk in order of their ages in their respective groupings with the eldest preceeding. The spouses of the siblings follow the siblings as a separate grouping but are arranged in the same order as their spouses.

The above order is utilized in Sandy Cove and Green Island Cove and perhaps in the Straits generally. In Savage Cove the order is different only in that the spouses of the children of the deceased siblings and the spouses of the siblings of the deceased walk with their respective husbands and wives instead of in groups behind them. The explanation given for this variation is that one of the early settlers used to say that when a person was in trouble his spouse should be with him and that the people of Savage Cove have this particular idea and therefore do it in this way. A reason given for the style in the other settlements is that those who are most concerned should be first and the "real" children and siblings are most concerned. In either system the unmarried children of the deceased will tend to

walk first with the surviving spouse despite the fact that they may
be the youngest. After the grandchildren come the congregation as a
whole. Other relatives may sometimes be included on the list. For
instance, at one funeral an uncle by marriage was put down "just to
be one of the bunch, he was the only uncle around."

When those who are not immediate relatives are on the list but,
as sometimes occurs, do not adhere to the taboos associated with
mourning the reaction may be . . . "It is hypocritical to read the
names of people who will be out on a time that night--it turns you."

The mourners wear black arm bands. The functionaries, the
bearers and those who make the coffin and dig the grave, have white
arm bands. The latter are not related to the deceased unless there
are not enough present at the funeral from which to choose non-relatives.
In such a case cousins might participate. One "wouldn't feel right"
about a mourner performing such tasks. An exception regarding relatives
being involved in this manner occurred at a funeral of an adolescent
boy. His father had the boys cousins bear the coffin as "it was the
last time they would be close to him." In the past men in mourning
wore black ribbons on their caps which hung down the back of the neck.

Topbearers and underbearers tear off their arm bands and throw
them into the grave "after the corpse"--sometimes mourners do this.
If they are not thrown into the grave they are thrown into the fire
in the kitchen stove.

The Problem of Origin

The relationship between the patrilocal extended family in the
Straits and local economy is manifest. That economic co-operation
should involve such a form is consonant with social anthropological
generalization on such phenomena.

> Patrilocal residence seems to be promoted by
> any change in culture or the conditions of life
> which significantly enhances the status, importance,
> and influence of men in relation to the opposite
> sex. Particularly influential is any modification
> in the basic economy whereby masculine activities
> in the sex division of labor come to yield the
> principal means of subsistence . . .   A similar
> effect tends to appear where men supplant women
> as tillers of the soil, often in consequence of
> harnessing their domestic animals to the plow.

> Even among hunters and gatherers the same result
> can be produced if a tribe moves into an area where
> game is plentiful and dependable, so that subsistence
> comes to depend primarily upon the chase rather than
> upon the collecting activities of the women (Murdock,
> 1949:206).

This quotation raises the question of the derivation of the patrilocal extended family in the Straits and in Newfoundland. Its distribution on the Island is at present unknown, although it is clear that it does and did occur in various areas. The lack of knowledge here, as well as the dearth of information about the folk culture of Newfoundland as a whole, demonstrates that in many areas much more is known about the lives of North American aborigines than of the contemporary residents. The publication of the work that has been done by the various anthropologists who worked in other parts of Newfoundland as Research Fellows of the Institute of Social and Economic Research of the Memorial University of Newfoundland will help fill this gap. This lack of data is also true of Europe. Messenger states . . .

> Most of the ethnographic research among folk
> peoples has been done in Latin America, Africa, and
> Asian communities. European anthropologists, who
> might have interested themselves in their own folk
> traditions given over historical circumstances, have
> been most concerned with studying primitive societies,
> especially those in the colonial territories of their
> respective nations. It is the folklorists, historians,
> economists, and sociologists who have documented
> European folk cultures, and their approach has been
> historical, primarily focused on the origin, survival,
> distribution, and comparison of cultural forms.
> Holistic community studies among European folk peoples,
> guided by the "disciplined use of the primitive society
> on a conceptual model" (Mead, 1953:653) are a recent
> innovation (1964:10).

It is no less difficult to obtain information regarding family structure in rural Ireland and England.

Whether such a structure is European in derivation or arose in the Strait of Belle Isle or elsewhere in Newfoundland is moot. I have not been able to obtain information on the family structure of those areas from which the first migrants came, at the time that they came. However, two factors make a hypothesis of a completely European origin unlikely. First of all it seems that the men who were recruited into the Newfoundland Fishery in its early days were not fishermen but West Country and Irish farmers (personal communication, Allan Williams) and while this in itself would not preclude their "possessing" the patrilocal extended family, it would represent a different economic system which at least in Western Ireland (Arensberg, 1937) produced a different structure. Second, the early settlers in Newfoundland worked on an individual basis as fishermen for planters who maintained large establishments. This would seem to preclude the family enterprise which could be effectively supported by the extended family.

It is possible that this type of organization originated in Newfoundland as an outgrowth of a commercial non-familial fishing enterprise in which men had individual shares, and what was an aspect of a non-familial commercial relationship was taken over as a part of the extended family structure.[12]

The fact that fishermen in non-familial commercial endeavors have shares is another parallel between the extended family and the non-familial fishing outfit and its nautical statuses of skipper and crew.

CHAPTER IV

THE DIVERSITY OF LABOR

The continuance of the patrilocal extended family is due to its economic
utility. This does not mean, however, that there is an absence of
sentiment regarding the existence of such a group: it is felt that
brothers should stay and work together and when this does not occur,
people tend to feel that it is because they could not agree rather than
because of economic advantages in separation. Nonetheless, brothers
sometimes leave such groups when they consider it to their own
advantage. Groups may prematurely split due to the imbalance of rewards
and efforts, aside from the regular segmentation which occurs.

Co-operative fishing endeavor forms the core integrating activity
of families. This activity provides the greatest income; and the
management and upkeep of fishing gear and structures, and the entire
process of fishing and drying ties together the labors and the interests
of the individuals involved. In a secondary sense sealing and other
hunting carried on by family members produces the same effect. Such
activities as relate to gardens and cows tend to be only household
affairs.

With fishing as a co-operative nexus individuals are able to
leave for temporary periods of labor outside the community and as long
as they contribute their income to the group as a whole the integrity
of the unit is maintained. In the past wood cutting was only seasonal
and carried on after the summer's fishing and so those individuals who
went would supplement their families' incomes without divorcing themselves
from the groups' primary endeavors or interests. The same is true of
those who now obtain temporary employment as laborers in Labrador or
elsewhere. It is, in fact, expected that men will leave for temporary
employment elsewhere when necessary, and this is not seen as a threat
to the structure of the local family. The family and households continue
to function at home and one of the men who has remained will take care of
the wood and other masculine chores.

As long as there is a core co-operative activity the group will
remain together in spite of independent temporary jobs taken by the

individual men. Therefore wood cutting on contract, where a family
member obtains a contract to provide so much wood and the men of the
family cut the wood as a group, can maintain the patrilocal extended
family as a core economic activity. In contrast, permanent employment
of men on an individual basis tends to break it up.

As an example of the first point we have Bellburns, a settlement
some 58 miles south of Savage Cove. Here the primary economic activities
are wood cutting from October until March and lobstering from about May
1st to July 12th (when it must legally cease) with preparations for
lobstering going on during April. What little cod fishing is done
begins the middle or even the first of July and may last until it is
time to go back into the woods. A man may obtain a contract to supply
so much pulp wood and he and his sons or brothers will carry it out.
It may be that the amount of wood to be obtained is sufficient for
the family group alone. If it is more than they can handle alone,
they may have others, usually relatives come in with them and be paid
a daily wage. In the past when lumbering was the prevalent type of
woodswork groups were larger, but cutting pulp wood requires fewer
men. It does happen sometimes that men will get individual contracts
for small lots of pulp wood and will "come together" and co-operate in
its cutting and hauling.

Lobstering is much more important than cod fishing in the area.
It is carried on in groups of two which is an efficient distribution
of labor for this enterprise, although one man could carry it on alone.
Such pairs work independently of the larger family group that they are
part of when cutting wood and the profits from their operations do not
go into the common family fund.

So, even though co-operative wood cutting as the major economic
activity may perpetuate the extended family, lobster fishing serves as
a divisive influence. We find the families not considered as much as
units as they are in the Straits. "They don't speak about groups the
same [as in the Straits], more as individuals, like Don and Herb or something like that." But patrilocal extended families still exist:
inheritance of capital goods and land is through males and parents live
with their youngest son, and his family.

Where labor is permanent individual wage work, or where there are individual shares in fishing enterprises involving large crews and owner- ship does not reside in the crew, one will tend to find only nuclear family organization. For example, in a community on the southern coast of Newfoundland studied by Louis Chiaramonte men ship out on trawlers as individual crewmen and only the nuclear family organization is present.

Life in the Straits means engaging in a wide variety of productive activities. First of all, men employ the various skills that go along with fishing including, among others, the ability to utilize a variety of fishing techniques, the knowledge of fish processing, the ability to make their own nets, boats and wharfs, and the capacity to navigate in a small open boat in a stormy, foggy stretch of ocean marked by strong and swift currents.

Hunting is also a necessity. I estimate that at least half of the meat eaten is game. Aside from the birds, rabbits and other animals taken for this purpose, seals are hunted in the spring for food, but primarily for their hides. In the past these were made into boots and other garments, but now the high price paid for skins makes sale the prime motive. To obtain the pelts the men walk out onto the moving ice of the Strait, which travels with the current, six miles up and six down, a dangerous venture requiring stamina and skill.

Until a few years ago many men would spend the fall of the year in the lumber camps supplementing the family income. This proved a source of security, for if the fishery was poor, a man could still earn something in the lumber woods. Woodsman's skills are also needed in obtaining the year's supply of firewood and in procuring the lumber required for building houses, wharves, sheds, and other construction-- and in the past, furniture. The new houses being built are contemporary style bungalows, very nicely done, and constructed without the aid of blue prints.

When dogs were the only source of winter transportation each man was also a carter and needed the handling skills required for driving these animals. Now, with snowmobiles, trucks and automobiles, it is necessary for men to have a not inconsiderable amount of mechanical skill as there are few professional mechanics in the area. The skills employed are derived from working with the inboard gasoline engines that have been in the area for perhaps forty or more years.

Hay for cows and horses used to be cut more extensively in the past then it is today and was provided from fenced fields in the community, meadows in the country, or even from the Labrador.

Women have in their domain, aside from all that is involved in cooking, sewing and care of the house and children, the milking and care of the cows, planting and tending the vegetable garden, and helping with the splitting, salting, and drying of the fish. They make many of the clothes and knit sweaters and stockings, but in the past they carded, spun and made almost all the clothes and worked hours into the night by the light of small oil lamps making seal skin boots for the family use and for sale.

This diversity of activity reflected the self-sufficiency of the area. The only indispensable food items brought in in the past were salt, molasses, white flour, salt pork, and salt beef. Nails, firearms, stoves, kitchen utensils, and rum were perhaps the only indispensable imported manufactured goods. With an increase in cash and the opening of roads in recent years more and more items of outside manufacture are becoming necessities. Manufactured goods have always been brought in to some degree, and items are ordered through the mail-order houses of Eaton's and Simpsons-Sears.

Since the coming of the road automobiles and trucks have made for a new orientation towards credit as time payments on these must now be regularly made despite fluctuations in local production and earnings. As local economy moves more and more away from a subsistence level, the chance becomes greater that one may have to do without what are becoming necessities. After a summer in which there has been a poor catch of fish one hears talk about how some people may lose the machines that they have obtained and how these are felt to be new and previously unnecessary burdens.

Although an increase in cash in the economy and the possession of more material goods and an easier life are valued--people frequently talk of how much harder times were in the past--one hears it said that "things were sweeter in the Straits in the past." People had less and so appreciated more what they did have. It was more difficult to travel and visiting outside the community was valued more.

The economic position of settlements in the Straits, as well as
that of Newfoundland in general, derives from the island's position as a
supplier of raw material (fish and wood pulp) to other parts of the world
rather than to an indigenous population. The island's original exploitati(
and consequent settlement were due to the exporting of fish, and until
the establishment of the wood pulp industry around the beginning of the
century, almost all income was from the export of fish. This resulted
in a thin scattering of population along the coast and no population in
the interior. Coastal settlement was determined by access to the fishery
which often meant life in isolated and uncomfortable places despite the
fact that in some areas separate winter houses were built in sheltered
spots (Newfoundland Fisheries Development Committee, 1953).

As production was for overseas consumption, there was no local
market development, no exchange of produce between local specialists such
as fisherman, farmer, artisan, and no differentiation near-at-hand
between rural and urban as the only urban center was St. John's until
the recent development of Grand Falls, Gander, Deer Lake and Corner Brook.
Commercial and political relations were primarily with the capital.

In the Straits the first economic link of the settlers with the
outside was the American schooners which took away the fish and furs
collected by the Genges (Richards, 1953a:18). After this stationers were
established on the Labrador side as mentioned previously.

About 60 years ago some of the Straits was served by a schooner
from Nova Scotia, the "Una." I am told it was owned by a Halifax
merchant named Mitchell and captained by a Captain DeWolfe (sp?). It
called every spring to deliver supplies and returned in the fall to
take off the fish in payment for them. This ship went to Green Island
Cove and Eddie's Cove as well as other communities. It supplied the
fishermen it served with most of their needs. The people served might
also shop at Flower's Cove for minor supplies. If the worth of the fish
came to more than the amount of the debt the captain paid in either
silver or gold. Much of this gold was cashed in sometime later when the
government offered $1.60 for each dollar of gold. The statement by one
old man that "The gold on the coast came from Nova Scotia and was taken
away by St. John's" indicates that it was not until later that fish was
typically sold to local merchants who sold it to firms on the east coast

of Newfoundland.

Fishing

Cod is the only commercial fish caught in the area. Some herring used to be taken, but it is no longer, and the local people are surprised to find that wolf fish (or ocean catfish) which they would never consider eating sells for a higher price than cod in the United States.

The cod arrive in the Strait around the middle of June. They follow the capelin as the latter move northeastward along the shore. Capelin are small smelt-sized fish which roll and spawn on the sandy beaches, much as do the grunion in California. Sandy Cove, the next settlement northeast, is where the people of Savage Cove obtain capelin for use in baiting their trawls.

The fishing season is short. It lasts only three to four weeks on the Newfoundland shore after which the men may carry it on from the Labrador side for another three or four weeks. The capelin leave the Newfoundland shore and move northeastward along the Labrador shore, thus taking with them the smaller cod which would be caught in the traps and removing themselves as bait for the trawls that could catch the remaining deeper water cod.

Before the fish arrive much time has been spent in preparing for the season. The new netting needed has been knit by the fishermen during the winter and spring. A man may knit fifty pounds of twine a year keeping up a cod trap. In May people are fitted out by the local merchants, obtain the fishing supplies needed for the season, repair all equipment and get it in order.

The cod trap is the primary fishing device. Not all families have traps but they are the means by which most fish are caught. The cod trap is essentially an oblong box of netting set just off-shore with its wide side parallel to the landwash [shore]. In the center of the side facing the shore is an opening and from this opening to the shore is stretched a net called the leader. As the cod skirt along the shore they encounter the leader and follow it into the doorway and once in the trap swim around and around unable to find their way out.

The trap is held up by five water tight kegs or sometimes by plastic buoys. Five rodes [lines running to grapnels] hold the trap in place. Each rode is attached to a graplin [grapnel] which is only with difficulty secured to the flat, even rock floor of the Strait. The two left hand rodes are called the vees, and the two right hand ones the corners. The upper right rode is designated the northeast corner and the lower right the southeast corner because going by local directional terminology, oriented by magnetic north, the top of the trap points north as the shore line runs northeast and southwest and the trap is set parallel to the shore.

The span line runs across the center of the trap at the top to help it keep its shape. The doorway or opening in which the fish enter is held apart by an iron bar or chain. The leader runs from this towards the shore and is held in place by short rodes called leader backers, its end is marked with a buoy and it is held to the landwash by a shore fast.

The trap proper is in three parts: the leader, the round, and the bottom. Each is a separate piece and these are sewn together when the trap is set out. The round makes up the sides of the trap and is of one piece. The top line of round, to which the linnet [netting] is attached, has corks attached to it to keep the linnet up in the water. This line is known as the head line or the heads, and the corresponding line at the bottom of the round is called the foot line or the foots. The foot line has stones or chain attached to keep it down in the water.

Aside from the rodes which run from the head lines to the graplins there are lines which run from the foots at the four corners to the four corner graplins. This keeps the foots steady in the tide. The latter are not used everywhere, but all traps in Savage Cove have them because of the strength of the tide. There may by buoy lines which are attached to the graplins to hold buoys marking their position.

The traps are from three to six fathoms deep and are placed in coves, if possible, or where the currents run less strong. The tides are stronger at the points and there is surf. If possible the trap is placed over a smooth cliff [solid rock bottom] or sandy bottom to keep the twine from tearing up. In Savage Cove there is but one tier of traps along the shore, but in adjacent Sandy Cove, which has a deep bight, there are three. The Savage Cove traps are strung along the entrance to the cove

Illustration II

Cod Trap

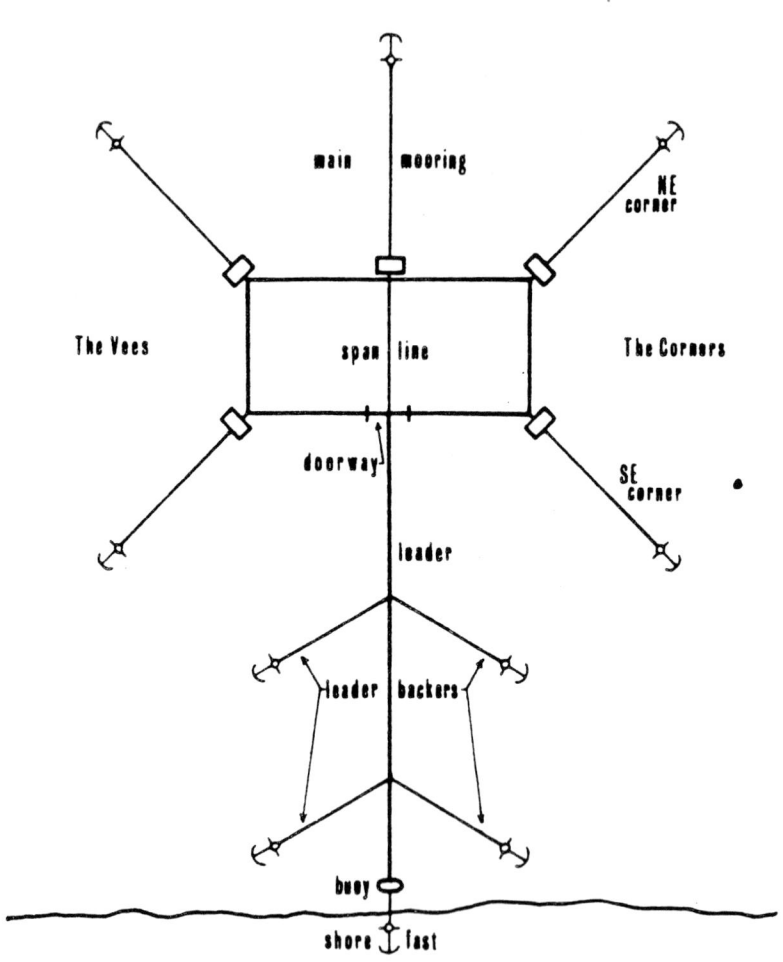

main mooring

NE corner

The Vees

span line

The Corners

doorway

SE corner

leader

leader backers

buoy

shore fast

⌘ graplin (grapnel)   ▢ kegs or buoys

ILLUSTRATION III

COD TRAP CORNER

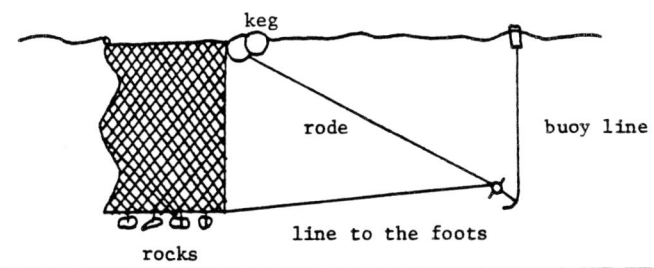

keg

rode   buoy line

line to the foots

rocks

from Savage Point to Yankee Point and some are placed in Middle Shoal
Cove. Most leaders are around 60 fathoms long and most traps are 16
fathoms long and six fathoms wide.

Traps are placed with the narrow end toward the tidal flow. Only
in sheltered areas with little tidal pull is it possible to have square
traps. At Flower's Cove there are some that are 70 fathoms in circum-
ference in contrast to the 40 to 45 fathoms of the oblong traps.

Traps can only be tucked [emptied] at the slack tide, at the point
when the tide is about to change and consequently exerts little pull.
At any other time the current is too swift for the operation to be
managed. As these points advance about one hour daily the time of
tucking varies daily. Traps are tucked twice each day to take advantage
of both tides. Traps are never tucked, nor is any other work done on
Sunday.

In tucking the trap the crew goes out in two small boats, the
motor boat, which is the trap boat, an open craft with a pointed bow,
rounded bottom and an angled counter, and powered by a small inboard
gasoline engine. The motor boat hauls a smaller unpowered punt which is
tied on at the stern. Arrived at the trap, the motor boat ties to the
landward side of the trap over the doorway and the crew proceeds to haul
up the bar which keeps the doorway open; thus, blocking the escape of
any fish during the tucking. The punt then proceeds to the end of the
trap which faces the direction from which the current is running and
disconnects the lines which run from the foots to the graplins thus

freeing the bottom of the trap on that side. The punt then moves along
that end of the trap and the men aboard it and those aboard the motor
boat proceed to haul netting out of the trap and stretch it between the
boats forming cuts [ridges] of linnet which restricts the fish. These
cuts continue to be made as the punt proceed towards and then along the
seaward side of the trap and accordingly the fish are forced into the
end of the trap which faces away from the flow of tide.

When the punt reaches the corner of the trap which is on the
seaward side and towards the direction of flow the motor boat comes
around to fasten onto the end of the trap away from the flow. The fish
have been forced into a small area at that end and they are then scooped
up with dip-nets and gathered in with the linnet as more and more of it
is taken into the motor boat.

The area in which each trap is moored is known as a berth. These
berths like land are obtained through patrilineal inheritance and
through establishing them in previously unused spots. In more populous
areas of Newfoundland the rights to berths are obtained each year by
lot with the most productive going to those who are lucky. Sandy Cove
has a system in which berths are used in rotation by the crews in the
community. In Savage Cove the hereditary rights to berths are respected,
everyone being aware just where everyone's rightful berth is, sometimes
by the aid of land markers which are sighted from the sea. If someone is
not using a berth, another can use it, but when the owner wants to use
it no one else will. The system runs entirely by informal sanction.

> We have no law here and if someone were to
> use your berth there would be nothing you could
> do about it. But no one does that.

Besides traps, trawls are also used. These consist of long lines
from which many short lines called suds bearing hooks are suspended.
They are moored under water by graplins and marked with buoys. Each line
has 75 to 90 suds placed three or four feet apart, is around 50 fathoms
long, and is set between 12 and 50 fathoms deep. Their hooks are baited
with capelin. The best place to place trawls is on the edge of banks.

ILLUSTRATION IV

TRAWLS

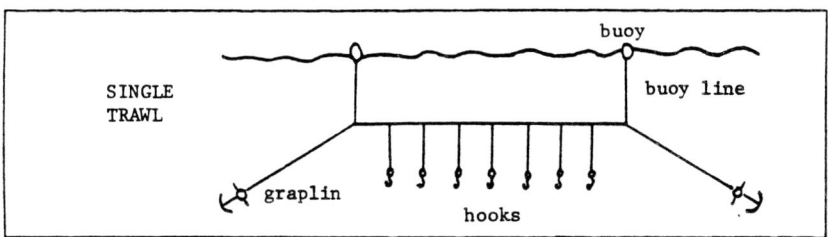

SINGLE
TRAWL

buoy

buoy line

graplin

hooks

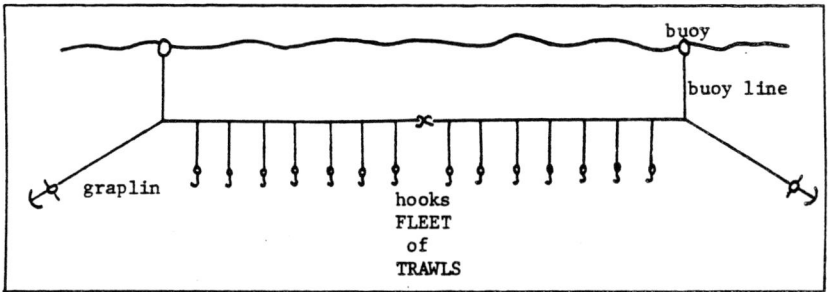

buoy

buoy line

graplin

hooks
FLEET
of
TRAWLS

Trawls are usually set out in fleets. A fleet of trawls usually consists of six to eight trawl lines joined together.

The capelin used for trawl bait is obtained at Sandy Cove as long as it lasts and later on the Labrador shore. Some can also occasionally be obtained at a bait depot on the Labrador while its small supply lasts.

Trawls are set out for extended periods of time, usually over-night, and then hauled, the catch removed and the hooks rebaited. In fly-and-set fishing the trawl is only left "to fish" for perhaps an hour after it is baited. It is then hauled and rebaited and set out again, this process being continued over and over. Ordinary trawling is more suited to a situation in which a fisherman has cod traps out and must attend them also; whereas, if one has no traps one can fly-and-set which requires constant attention while in process. An advantage of fly-and-set fishing is that when fish are not plentiful one can try different spots easily. An advantage of ordinary trawling is that the trawl is "working for you all the time it is out there."

98

In hauling a trawl the fishing boat is placed perpendicularly to the trawl line which is pulled up by means of a buoy line and passes across the boat from gunwhale to gunwhale. One fisherman pulls on the line and as he does so the boat moves slowly sideways along it. As the suds are taken into the boat this man takes the fish off the hook and a second man then rebaits the hook which then moves back into the water as the boat passes along the line. In fly-and-set fishing one of the graplins is lifted into the boat and the line is baited and coiled into a tub as the fish are taken off.

In jigging (fishing with a handline) the Straits fisherman uses a jigger of lead in the shape of a capelin with two hooks protruding from the forward end. This is attached to a line wound around a small frame. The line is unwound from the frame and the jigger dropped overboard unbaited. The line is then jerked violently so as to lure the cod into taking it. For jigging, as for trawling the best place is at the edge of a bank.

Gill nets have begun to be used in recent years. These are set out and the fish catch in them. Larger fish are caught in them than in the cod traps.

The three major fishing techniques are cod traps, trawls and jiggers with some use of gill nets. Everyone who uses traps uses trawls and jigs from time to time and those who have no traps trawl and jig or only jig. If one has a trap and the amount of fish obtained in it is sufficient to keep one busy no other techniques are used, and similarly, if one has no trap and relies primarily on a trawl it is always possible to try jigging if the trawl proves unsatisfactory. There are few who rely on jigging alone. Usually the greatest catches of fish are obtained with a trap, the next greatest with the trawl, and the fewest with the jigger. Trawling takes more work then using a trap. Traps are tucked twice per day, but if you trawl only "you're hauling a trawl all day"--a good outfit for trawling is two six or seven line fleets per boat.

After the season is over on the Newfoundland side most of the men that go over to the Labrador from Savage Cove and Sandy Cove fish in Schooner Cove which is in L'Ance au Loup Bay. They camp out about a mile from the settlement of L'Ance au Loup and some build tilts [small

shacks] to stay in. Many finish the season there but others follow
the fish northeast along the coast of West St. Modest. The government
has built a bunk house and wharf there for Newfoundland fishermen.
It holds fifty to sixty men and costs one dollar per week to stay in.
Life is particularly hard when engaging in the fishery on the Labrador.
The men must work long hours, prepare their own food, as well as
frequently journey back and forth across the Strait.

Although some go over merely to jig or trawl many take their
cod traps over. The tides are stronger on the Labrador shore and the
traps are placed in water that is shallower than the trap, as otherwise
the current would pull them under water. There are no berths on the
Labrador and very few of the people living there use them. Whoever
gets there first sets his trap where he pleases. Gill nets, which began
to come in about five years ago, are used largely on the Labrador
although some people use them at Anchor Point and Flower's Cove. Many
take them over to Labrador instead of cod traps: bigger fish are
obtained and using them is not as hard work, and as the water is rough
they can be put in places where traps cannot. The size of the fish
caught in the net compensates for the greater number of smaller fish
that would be taken in a trap. The gill nets are put in 15 to 20 fathoms
of water where one finds bigger cod. Trap fish are the smallest obtained.

Some fishing devices which are no longer used in the area are
handlines, dappers, seines, and cod nets.

Handlines[1] were reportedly not used in the area but were used
around St. Anthony and Quirpon. Here the groundlead [a piece of lead
six to seven inches long] is attached to the end of a line. There are
two hooks attached to the lead, one on each end. There are also two
hooks, one attached to each of two suds two to two and one-half feet long,
which are suspended from a hole which is bored through one end of the
ground lead. All hooks were baited.

A dapper was a piece of lead about four inches long with a hook
at one end. The dapper hook was smaller than a jigger hook. It was
baited and put overboard on an eight to ten fathom line. Two of these
devices would be used, one at each side of the boat. This was done with
the boat moored. In contrast, when jigging the boat drifts. This device
was used in the Straits.

Seines were used before cod traps were introduced. These were
about 80 fathoms long and eight fathoms deep. One end would be put
overboard and then the rest would be laid in a circle around a school
of fish. When the ends were joined the foots were pulled aboard first.
As this was done a trouncer, an iron ring about the size of a jacket
bow with 15 or 20 iron rings attached to it, was thrown in to frighten
the fish back toward the perimeter of the net so as to keep them from
escaping through the hole formed by the taking up of the foots. Seining
was carried on before cod traps came in. After their introduction
seines were cut up and made into cod traps.

In the past nets known as cod nets were used. These were like
gill nets but were deeper, about two fathoms deep; whereas, gill nets
are about one fathom deep. Like gill nets they were moored on both
ends. They were in use until about 12 years ago, and were placed in
four to seven fathoms of water.

At the present time all the fish caught in Savage Cove is sun
dried, although in the past some fish has been sold salt bulk, salted
but not dried. When the fishermen return with their catch it is
pitched up onto the end of the fishing stages as the first step in its
processing. If it happens that so many fish are caught in the traps
that there is a backlog in the "splitting" a large catch may be kept
overnight in a cod bag. This is a large bag shaped net into which the
cod are put after the trap is tucked. It is then towed in from the
trap and tied on to the fishing stage.

The stage is a small wharf extending from the landwash. They are
built far enough out into the cove to enable a motor boat to be tied to
the end at low tide. As the water is quite "shoal" in Savage Cove this
means that the stages extend some considerable distance. Nonetheless, at
very low tides even the ends of some of the stages at the bottom of the
cove cannot be reached in a motor boat. Most stages are supported by
posts which are connected by horizontal timbers to form cribs. Heavy
rocks are placed on the beams which make up the bottom of these cribs
and are confined by timbers which form the sides.

These require regular maintenance and repair particularly in the
spring as the harbor ice tends to push and twist the structures out of
line. Another form of support for stages is called hodges or cross

wharves. Here the wharf is laid upon beams which are held in the angles
formed by crossed supports. This is used usually in temporary structures.

The floor of a stage, or the bedding is made up of boards which
lie perpendicularly upon two sets of beams that rest on the cribbing and
run the length of the structure.

There are three sheds that are associated with each stage. They
are the splitting stage, the inside stage, and the store. The splitting
stage is a small structure built on the end of the stage. After the
fish are pitched onto the stage they are individually put through a hole
in the side of the splitting stage and slide down a short shute into a
bin inside. They are taken from the bin and placed upon the splitting
table where their heads, backbones and entrails are removed. The entrails
are thrown out a hole in the side of the structure to fall into the water;
whereas, the livers, which are saved to be rendered into oil, are
dropped through a hole in the splitting table into a bin underneath.

The split fish are carried to the inside stage, at the other end
of the wharf in a wheel barrow. There they are salted and stacked in
tiers (made into salt bulk). Then, as time permits, they are later
taken out, washed, and placed on the beaches to dry in the sun.

Women and children help in the processing of the fish. The women
help split, salt and wash the fish and the children help in heaving the
fish out of the boats onto the stage and lifting them from the stage
through the window of the splitting stage. They also may take wheel
barrow loads from the splitting stage to the inside stage and help with
the washing of the fish. It is the women and children, with the help
of some of the men, who tend the fish out on the beach when it is drying.
Before the road came in flakes were in use, and are still used in some
settlements, for drying fish. These were platforms supporting evergreen
boughs on which the fish were placed to dry. They were near the stores,
but with trucks it is just as convenient to transport the fish to the
nearby beach and not have the trouble of keeping up flakes.

Lumbering

The company lumber camps are no longer in existence. They ceased operations a few years ago. One is told that the company which operated the camps closed them because a union which was forming demanded improved living conditions in the camps, and the company, feeling that these would raise costs unduly, closed them. Logging in the area today centers around Main Brook on the opposite side of the Peninsula. This community has grown up in recent years as a result of pulp wood cutting. There is still good wood to be cut on the eastern side of the Peninsula; whereas, the western side has largely been cut over. In order to cut wood now in the area one must either reside in Main Brook and environs or, if one is not living permanently in that area, board with a local family or with the one man who runs a cook house. Men are not allowed to "shack" by themselves in the woods, nor are there company camps.

Various families from the Straits and Savage Cove have moved permanently to Main Brook to work at pulp wood cutting as their primary economic activity. They are able to live there because they can work "at the wood" for a longer season than the fall activity which characterized the participation of most men in the Straits.

Most men in the Straits express regret at the disappearance of the company camps. They consider that it was a dependable means of supplementing earnings from fishing, and if the fishery was poor a man could always have gone into the woods to make a go of it. The loss in income due to the disappearance of the camps seems to have been somewhat compensated for by the unemployment insurance and welfare payments that have come in, in recent years. Since fishermen are eligible for unemployment insurance they may receive payment throughout the winter based upon the number of fish caught during the fishing season.

One detriment of the lumber camps was that many people "let their fishing gear go down"—did not keep it in good repair. In the usual pattern for a family actively engaged in fishing at that time those men not needed to dry fish went to cut pulp early in the fall later to be followed by most of the other when the fish was dried. A large catch needed many to dry the fish and no one might go; but if it were small many might go. The fact that money could be obtained in the woods in the fall plus the effort and organization involved in carrying on both activities resulted in a certain lack of activity in the fishery. Before the camps came into existence there were some men who would get contracts to cut wood.

Men used to travel about twenty miles to reach the lumber camps in the area. Each camp had a foreman known as the skipper. He kept the time, blazed the areas that were to be cut with the help of the second hand, and was the general supervisor. His assistant, the second hand, placed the men in the areas they were to cut. Either the skipper or the second hand would come around once a day to see how each man was doing. This, to one informant, was considered a way in which the men were looked after--"you might have been hurt and [otherwise] no one would know it." The use of such terms of status are more indicators of the nautical orientation of the culture. The men were referred to as "all hands."

The woods to be cut would be blazed off into strips 50 feet wide and be of any length, depending on growth and the amount to be cut. Each of these strips had a branch road running down the center of it and each strip lay perpendicular to the main road. First the main road would be cut and then the blazes indicating the margins of the strips would be made every 50 feet. Each man was assigned to his strip.

There is "good wood" and "bad wood." Black spruce is a bad wood although it is supposed to be the best wood for pulp. It grows crooked and short and is to be found "in the bog," that is, on the edge of the mesh [marsh] and sometimes in the mesh. A good wood is vir [fir] which is to be found on the rudges [ridges] or high ground.

The wood was cut into junks[2] [chunks] four feet long and piled in landings to be measured by the scaler. When cutting, a man would stay in his strip until he got to the end. In the lumber woods the men worked a ten-hour day. Breakfast was at six o'clock and the cook would be up by half past four. Work began at seven when the men left for the strips they were cutting. There were two lunches, ten and two, lunch boxes being taken along. Supper was at six o'clock and after supper the men went to the bunkhouse. There they often sang songs, danced, played cards, and told stories. "Bunker-down" time was at nine or half past nine.

Next to the bunk house was the cook house. It was around 40 feet long and there were two tables in it, each about 20 feet long and placed side by side. The men's entrance was on the side opposite the cook's end which was partitioned off, but there was no door. Inside the cook's end there were two stoves on one side of the entrance and shelves on the other. In back of this area there was a pantry in which the cook would keep bread, buns, cakes and also stores.

Aside from the cook there were two men called cookees. They helped the cook, got wood, and water for the cook house, and scrubbed the floor and served meals.

Cutting, the chop, could start about the first of September, though it has started as early as the 15th of August, and lasts until around Christmas. Most of the men would return then but a few would remain for the "haul off." Here the wood was pulled to the brooks by horses or, in later years, tractors. This ended in May and then "the drive" would begin when it was driven along the brooks to the sea to be loaded for shipment abroad.

Sealing

Sealing arouses much enthusiasm in the Straits, particularly in Savage Cove whose men have a reputation for being eager to get out on the ice. The primary quarry are harp seals, but sometimes hood seals are encountered and taken. Both species migrate seasonally through the Strait of Belle Isle. The harps give birth on the ice in March and the men walk out on the ice seeking the young and the mothers. Later in the season when the ice begins to break up and boats can get through they are pursued in the water and shot. On the ice they are clubbed with bats.

When the men go out on the ice they go in groups of two to ten. A man could go by himself but it would be dangerous as there would be no one to pull him out if he fell in. The news of the seals being seen in the Strait may come via the radio reports of the weather stations in the area or reports of others who have been out and spotted them. In going out after them one must first cross the standing ice which is locked to the land and extends one half to two thirds of a mile into the Strait. The running ice which the sealer must get onto fills most of the Strait and is composed of tightly packed pans which move up and down with the current for approximately six miles in either direction. When the wind blows toward the Newfoundland shore it may leave a "lake" of open water on the Labrador side and vice versa. The gap between the standing ice and the running ice, or the line where the one is pressed against the other, is called the _gutter_ by the shoreman and the _running joint_ by the sealers aboard the steamers which engage in the seal hunt. The most dangerous time in sealing is crossing the gutter for the pans of the running ice have a tendency to turn over as they are pressed along the standing ice. Other dangers include the necessity of having to leap from pan to pan, being attacked by a hood seal, and the ever present danger of drifting out to sea if changes in the wind and tide move the ice away from shore. Even a small gap opened in the ice will prevent a return home. There are various cases of men stranded out on the ice floes overnight and surviving the cold by step-dancing and burning seal fat for warmth.

One only goes out on the running ice during the "up" tide which is the rising tide that flows southwest (locally west). During this tide the current pulls toward the Newfoundland side of the Strait and holds the ice against the land, at least along the southwestern half of that shore. The ice at that end also tends to be held by Flower's Ledges which project into the Strait at Nameless Cove. However, beyond the Strait south along the coast the "land falls back" (dips more to the south) and the current no longer has this effect. The "down" tide, the falling tide which flows northeast (locally east) pulls toward the Labrador side and loosens the ice on the Newfoundland side or carries it away from the standing ice.

Wind direction is also of significance in going out onto the ice. One can go out when the wind is northwest (north locally), west (northwest), or north (northeast) as this pushes the ice shoreward. A southeast (south) wind tends to blow the ice offshore and the ice is to be avoided then as it should be during a southwest (west) wind and a northeast (east) wind, although some will go out during the latter two when the ice is tight. On the Labrador the opposite wind is wanted to what is desired on the Newfoundland shore for the same effect.

The men wear _rackets_ [snow shoes] while on the ice for good traction and to enable them to cross patches of slob ice, small pieces of ice which are pressed together. In order to be supported by it on snowshoes there must be a strong wind pressing it in toward the land. The snowshoes used are locally made and are broad and short for this purpose. The spruce bats or **gaffs** which are carried are about six feet long and have a gaff consisting of a point and a hook in one end. A hunting knife is a necessity along with a steel, for the knife is easily dulled by striking the seals' ribs in skinning. A six fathom rope to which the pelts are tied and hauled home is also taken along.

A seal is killed by a blow on the head. If this does not kill the seal it is struck on the throat. In skinning one cut is made down the belly from mouth to rear flippers, another is made around the neck, and then cuts are made around the flippers and the pelt is then pulled off the carcus. The fat and skin are taken off together—this is known as the pelt—the skin referring only to the skin without the fat.

The number of seals that a "hearty" man is said to be able to pull in off the ice is twenty and I have heard of men pulling in twenty-five. Hauling them back is extremely hard work and I have heard men say that it was the hardest work they ever touched. The pelts are tied with the head of each succeeding skin at the front flipper hole of the previous as to make for better slipping on the ice.

The young of the harp and the hood seal are born on the ice. At birth the young of the harp are pure white and in the past these had more commercial value than the adult seal, but now the opposite is true. The harp seals, whose name is derived from the shape of the saddle on the back of the adult, are locally distinguished as follows in terms of age and attendant markings:

> Whitecoat—for about the first twenty days; all
> white except the eyes and nose.
>
> Ragajack—(from "ragged jacket") skin buyers call
> it a shedder; has black spots on belly.
>
> Beater—first year; black back, grey belly, some
> black spots on belly.
>
> Bedlamer—second year; larger than a beater but
> much the same color.
>
> Turner—three to four years; can barely see the
> saddle of the adult on back.
>
> Old Harp—adult seal; saddle on back and no black
> spots on belly.

Male hoods or harps are referred to as <u>dogs</u> and females <u>bitches</u>. Only some harp bitches will bother the hunters when they go after the whitecoats and may try to bite if the hunter gets near them or may even come after him. In this case it may be necessary to kill the bitch or at least stun her by hitting her on the nose rather than on the front of the skull. The whitecoats will not move.

Hoods are "surlier" than harps and will always try to protect their young. They have a "hood" of skin on their heads and "puff it up when you go after them." Hoods are differentiated by age only into <u>young hoods</u>, the current year's seals, and <u>old hoods</u>, which are the rest.

Seals are also taken in nets and in <u>seal frames</u> which are anchored immediately off shore. At Anchor Point seal nets are employed which are of shallow depth and have tops which lie below the surface so that the ice may pass over them. Their advantage is that they may be "fished" before the ice has completely cleared off the shore, whereas the following are limited in use to the short period between the time the ice leaves and cod fishing begins. In most of the settlements in the Straits the heads of the seal nets come to the top of the water. All extend perpendicularly out from the shore and are designed to trap the seals as they skirt along the shore. The seals become entangled ("mesh") in the nets and drown.

The basic pattern is displayed above. It consists of a net running straight out from the shore with a "hook" at the end where the net angles sharply back towards the land. There are variants of this pattern which display an extra hook parallel to and behind the first, or maintain a "v" shaped indentation in the center.

The seal frame is a more elaborate affair than the net. It consists of three nets set at right angles so as to form a three sided enclosure with the shore making up the fourth side. One of the side nets is so arranged that it can be lowered to the bottom to be raised when a seal swims over it to enter the enclosure. The latter, the <u>enter net</u>, is operated by means of a capstan on shore. There is usually a small tilt called a <u>watch house</u> by the capstan, in which a man sits and waits for a seal to enter the frame. When this occurs he raises the enter net and fires at the seal with a rifle.

I do not know of seal frames existing south of Anchor Point nor outside of both sides of the Strait of Belle Isle. Canon Richards (1953b:15-16) states that they were invented locally by the Genges as well as describing them and their operation.

> At Anchor Point, too, thousands of old harps after traversing St. Barbe's Bay would round the point and pass on. This so aggravated the old Genges, that they resolved on a plan of securing some of the eastward bound herd. The strongest hemp twine was procured, and netted large enough to entangle the old harp. The seal frame was thus invented. This trap, consisting of sufficient linnet to extend hundreds of fathoms, was fastened to the shore, run straight off from the land perhaps forty or fifty fathoms, then carried at right angles parallel to the shore, and formed a huge netted box into which the unsuspecting seal would swim. From the end of this enclosure a barrier of twine was carried to the shore, and weighted with lead to sink it to the bottom. To this barrier was fastened a power- ful capstan where a man kept a keen watch for passing seals. These usually run in schools numbering any- where up to hundreds. A school may be seen a quarter of a mile away, to dive, and perhaps not be seen any more. The skilled watchman will wait until he is pretty sure the school--or some of them--have passed over the sunken barrier into the frame. He then runs to the capstan, heaves up the barrier, and hopes for good results.
>
> After he has to wait in uncertainty for many minutes, as the old harp is no fool, although unable to cope with his mortal enemy. At length, compelled to come to the surface to breathe, a head pops up here, another there, and the watchman counts ten, fifteen, sometimes fifty at one time. Now the barbarous battle begins, and a boat with men and guns goes into the frame, and when the seals appear the men riddle them with bullets. The object is to force them to mesh. This the poor doomed seal is too intelligent to do until, frightened by the noise, or wounded by bullets, he makes a last desperate dash for his life, and is caught in the net, where unable to come to the surface to breathe, in a short while he drowns.

The last few years have seen a great rise in the commercial value of seal skins and this is the primary incentive for their being hunted today. However, in the past they were also taken for local use as seal skin boots were the usual footwear. The skin was also used in making dog whips, the fillings of rackets, and occasionally a pair of skin pants or a nunny bag [nap sack]. Now few skin boots are seen. The seal skin to make them is almost too valuable for local use and women are now

ILLUSTRATION V

SEAL FRAME

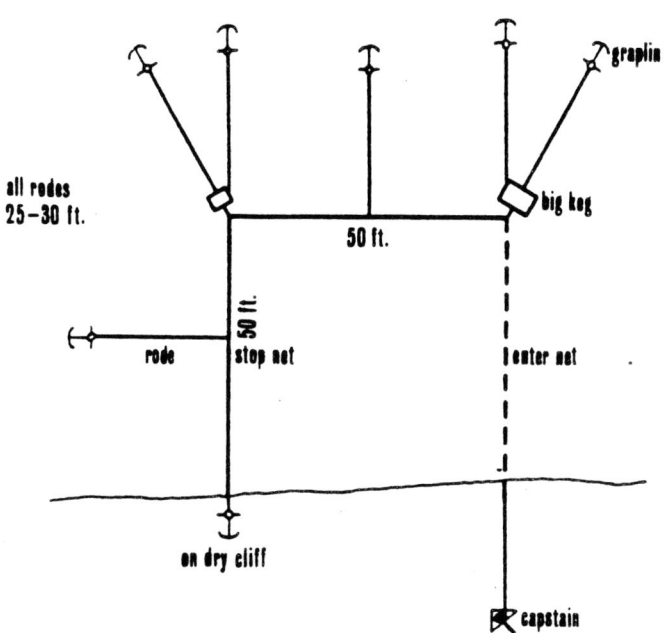

all rodes
25-30 ft.

50 ft.

big keg

graplin

50 ft.

rode

stop net

enter net

on dry cliff

capstain

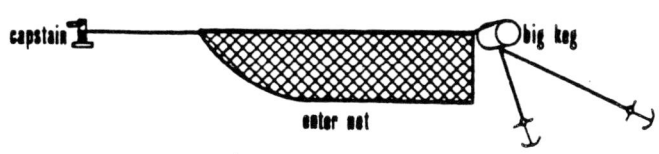

capstain

enter net

big keg

relieved of the tedious effort of their manufacture. In the past the
blubber of the seal was of more commercial value than the skin.

Hunting

Arctic hares and sea birds constitute a large portion of local
meat intake. The rabbits [arctic hares] turn brown in the summer and
white in the winter and are usually taken in slips, small loops of wire
set over their runs. A man may go out alone to teel slips [set snares]
but sometimes a party may go out for a number of days. The single man
will teel his slips out over a certain section and is careful to
remember the location of each one, sometimes with the aid of blazes,
and periodically makes his rounds of the traps. Each slip is set high
enough off the ground so the unwary rabbit will put his head through
and strangle. The rabbits are eaten fresh and also bottled [home
canned] for future use as are birds. Like birds they are a customary
soup meat.

Various birds that migrate along the coast are shot. Most of
these are murrs, which are called turrs locally. These are black and
white sea birds distantly related to the auks which were found on the
nearby Funks. Tinkers, almost identical to the murrs, and puffins, stumpy
creatures with multicolored parrot-like beaks are also taken. Kittiwakes
(tickle-ace) are also taken and in the past gulls were sometimes eaten.
Blinds (gazes) are used along the landwash. These are walls of stone
slabs and driftwood behind which the hunters lie, but most seabirds are
shot from boats. In the past, when food was scarce, little snow buntings
were sometimes netted or shot with buckshot while feeding on corn
scattered in a trench dug through a snow drift.

From Sandy Cove and northeastward one can see rows of owl trees
or owl bushes along the open shoreline and the rise beyond. During the
winter the Great Snowy Owl migrates from the Labrador and fishes out
over the ice at night coming to roost during the day on the Newfoundland
shore. Small trees are cut down and placed in open areas along the
shore. They are shored up at the base with rocks and sticks and their
branches are trimmed leaving a few at the top which are cut back and
tied together to form a level bed upon which horizontal twigs are
secured. On top of this platform a small animal trap is placed and
secured to the tree. When the owl alights its feet are caught in the trap,

and it is usually found by the owner of the tree hanging head downward
by the line which secures the trap. It is dispatched, if still alive,
with a stick.

Some muskrats are taken for their skins and for food, but few
beaver or otters are captured. At one time a good number of foxes were
taken and great amounts are reported as having been paid for some of the
pelts. In the past there were caribou in the area but they have long
been killed off. Some moose, introduced into Newfoundland in 1904, are
still in the area.

Gardens

Gardens are the responsibility of the women although one of the
men may assist in the digging, and children help in planting, weeding,
and harvesting. Gardens are put in in late May or early June--as soon
as the snow melts off the plots. Cabbage plants are started earlier
indoors in tin cans and kept in the windows for transplanting.
Potatoes, turnips, carrots, beets, and in at least one community
rhubarb, are grown. The plots are usually near the house of the household using it, but sometimes two or three households of an extended
family together use one plot.

The potato beds run in strips three to three and one-half feet
wide. Before planting they may be raked over to remove rocks, sticks,
and debris. To make the beds as straight as possible their edges are
marked by a piece of twine stretched between two stakes. Between the
beds running their length are strips of earth from six to twelve inches
wide. This earth is loosened with a mattock at planting, manure is
spread over the bed, and potato "seeds" are put in three or four across
in rows about a foot apart, and the loose dirt from the strips is shoveled
over them. Small seed [the other vegetables] beds are made by first
turning over all the ground to be used with mattocks and shovels. Beds
are marked out with stakes and twine. Seeds are then put in, manure is
spread and dirt from strips separating the beds spread over that. Both
cow manure, and fish manure (capelin) are used.

The gardens' fences are composed of a series of vertical sticks
or boards nailed to two horizontal pieces. These are made in sections
about five to six feet long and each is wired to posts sunk in the ground

with one section so fastened as to make one end easy to unwire and this serves as a gate. Horses and cows are often a problem during the growing season as they will sometimes knock down the fences to get at the crops.

Cows are milked twice a day while they are producing enough milk to warrant it. As soon as it becomes old enough to keep, the yearly calf is killed for its meat.

As the government contributes a significant amount to the incomes of the area it is necessary to view its contribution along with that of the various types of production. Table I gives a breakdown of incomes of six householders in Savage Cove which range from around the highest to around the lowest in the community. The table represents the 1963 season which was a particularly good one for both fish and seals. The price of cod has now increased to around $20 per quintal (112 pounds). The amount of fish cited as caught is that part of the crews' catches to which each man is entitled. Two men on the list are sharemen and so their fish is half the amount they would have if they had been share-holders. Similarly, the values of cod oil and seals stated are those parts of the value of the total catch that accrue to individual share-holders. Sharemen do not receive a share of the oil, nor are they involved in sealing operations.

As can be seen from the table total net fishing income is only part of individuals' incomes. Family allowance payments are received by all those with children and unemployment benefits provide a considerable portion of incomes for those who have earned them.

> The method of assessing a man's eligibility for Unemployment benefits is based on having a sufficient number of 'stamps,' which are issued him by the buyer each time he sells or ships codfish, lobsters, salmon, or seal. 'Stamps' vary in value depending on that amount of fish sold above the minimal requirements to get the lowest-valued stamp. The higher the value of the stamp, the more money a man receives in each Unemployment cheque (received every two weeks during the period of unemployment) and the greater the number of stamps, the longer Unemployment is received. Benefits may be drawn up to a maximum of 20 weeks, and may be up to 36.00 [dollars] per week for those with the highest-value stamps (Faris, 1966:143).

In the Straits unemployment benefits are seen as being the right of fishermen, whereas welfare payments are seen in a different light, at least, by those who do not receive them. Welfare, or "the dole," is disdained by men who are self-sufficient, and old men will take pride in their never having been on it, even in times of great deprivation. Among those who derive little from productive efforts welfare payments plus family allowance make up almost all of the income.

Family allowances are given to all families with children in Canada, six dollars per month for younger children and eight for older children. An economic survey done in 1963 in the Strait of Belle Isle (Wise, 1963: table XXIX) gives the percentage breakdown of derivation of incomes of heads of households, thirty-five household heads of various communities of the area being sampled. Of these only 45% of total income, on the average, was derived from fishing. Four percent of income was derived from welfare payments, 16% from family allowance, 19% from unemployment insurance, and 16% from other income, presumably wages. With 39% of income coming from government funds it is easy to appreciate the economic effect of Confederation upon Newfoundland. Since before unification little was available in the way of relief funds or even local government projects. However, in the past some of the funds now derived from the government would have been made up of money earned in the lumber woods. The average unemployment insurance benefit of this sample of 35 was $351. Family allowance was $296, welfare payments, $76, and "other income," $297, making a total non-fishing income of $1,856 (Wise, 1963: table XXVII).

Fishing expenses listed Table I cover such diversities as gas, oil, grease, fishing equipment, salt (on which the government gives a rebate) and truckage--carrying the dried fish from the storehouse to one of the government wharves for loading on schooners. Despite the fact that most families grow a substantial amount of vegetables most must buy at least additional potatoes to see them through the winter. The amounts listed on the table under worth of crops include hay for cows and horses minus those expenses involved in making gardens, such as fertilizer.

The income of a company consists of the income of its share-holders plus that of the sharemen. Only 45% of the average householders income derives from company fishing activities, and presumably the 16% which makes up "other income" is divided by the earners through the company.

This means that at least 39% of incomes are derived from outside the
company--namely from the government. Actually more of each family's
subsistance than this comes from non-company activities such as
gardening and dairying. According to Wise (1963:table XXXII) $39 was
the worth of the average number of potatoes grown, $76 of hay, with an
average of $147 per household for all crops. Average milk production
came to $154 with butter, $96.3. In addition to this is the value of
game obtained in hunting.

TABLE I

Household Incomes

Fisherman	Cod	Cod Liver Oil	Seals	Fishing Gross	Fishing Expenses	Fishing Net	Unemployment	Family Allowance	Wages	Welfare	Total Income	Worth of Groups*	Worth of Milk and Butter**
1.	169 qu. @ $17.00 $2,873	$28	$492	$3,393	$356	$3,037	15 wks. @ $26 $720	$423	$ 100	—	$4,248	$212	$716
2.	74 qu. @ $17.00 $1,258	—	540	1,798	72	1,726	20 wks. @ $20 390	216	—	—	2,332	102	—
3.	85 qu. @ $17.50 $1,488	—	—	1,488	250	1,238	20 wks. @ $20 400	408	—	—	2,046	42	140
4.	126 qu. @ $16.50 $2,079	18	—	2,097	401	1,696	18 wks. @ $36 648	720	$1000	—	4,064	60	226
5.	20 qu. @ $15.50 $310	—	—	310	share men	310	—	336	—	441	1,087	42	—
6.	15 qu. @ $17.50 $262	—	—	262	143	119	—	624	—	516	1,259	81	414
7.	50 qu. @ $16.50 $825	—	—	825	share men	835	12 wks. @ $36 432	72	—	—	1,329	14	—

* minus expenses and including hay
** minus cost of purchased food

CHAPTER V

INTERPERSONAL RELATIONS

Working together is certainly an integrating factor in extended families. Each individual contributes his efforts to the group and gains in return not only the satisfaction of his or her material and general emotional needs, but also a feeling of worth and identity through group participation. These are reasons why individuals co-operate: in co-operating they gain material and emotional satisfactions. Looked at from a more basic view, they must work together with relative harmony in order to exist. I say relative harmony because strife and discomfort are, of course, part of all social life, among primitives, peasants, in cities, and in rural fishing communities. In the Straits we find a way of life which, despite periodic minor conflicts and a high degree of competitiveness among the men of the area, is characterized by co-operation and warm personal relationships.

What this chapter is concerned with, then, are the ways in which harmony is achieved in a competitive community with little formal authority. What will be pointed out particularly is the general mode or style of interpersonal relations which makes for harmony in such a social setting.

All societies must be so arranged that their members are able to proceed in their own interests without unduly disrupting social life. Such major disruptions do, of course, occur, but in most cases they merely punctuate the relatively tranquil rather than become continuous.[1] Societies do vary in the extent to which the individual is expected to seek his own self interest and the degree to which he is intimidated by group coercion. Nonetheless, in all societies there must be some techniques by which individuals can articulate their own actions with those of their fellow men.

In societies characterized by intimate face-to-face relations the need for such mechanisms is particularly acute. This is so because the individual's total self tends to be immersed in a single uniform social milieu and how he performs in all his roles may be known about by most members of his local society. In urban society the individual interacts

with various groups and his behavior in one need not be congruent with
his actions in the others.

> Merton's concept of the role-set (Merton, 1957)
> also has application here. Merton points out that
> roles are often part of a set, for example--
> teacher, pupil, head, school, governor, parent.
> In such a role set, each role-other may have
> different role-expectations in relation to the
> teacher. The incumbent of the teacher-role can only
> succeed in meeting their conflicting expectations
> if the situation lacks what Merton calls transparency.
> That is to say it is necessary that one role-other
> should neither be present nor know of the teacher's
> behaviour to another role-other in the set. Trans-
> parency is more likely to arise in the rural than
> in the non-rural situation. This gives rise to
> special conflict reducing rituals and practices in
> the rural area. In the non-rural area the same is
> achieved by spacial and social segregation
> (Frankenberg, n.d.:11-12).

As we have seen the entire Strait area is characterized by
intimacy and familiarity. There is little mobility in the Straits and
a person can expect to spend his entire life in much the same social
milieu. Thus, techniques for maintaining his integrity while pursuing
his course through social proceedings with intimates are particularly
important. Egalitarianism is also significant here as it precludes
interaction in terms of a facade of superordinate and subordinate
relationships: one must get on "man to man" with no formalities of
position that would make for the isolation of social distance.

A traditional lack of formal political sanction also makes such
mechanisms necessary. Except for a recently established and fairly
inactive community council at Flower's Cove, there is no local government. With the coming of the road the RCMP has had access to all
communities throughout the year and the magistrate makes periodic trips
into the area to try those cases that come up. Before the roads the
area was completely isolated for six months of the year, and the jural
and police powers of the province were remote from the affairs of most
settlements, even though before Confederation there was a ranger
stationed at Flower's Cove, and at one time there was a small court
house established there.

This means that disharmony is a local matter and traditionally one could expect little or no help or protection of an external impartial force, nor was there any local formal method of settling disputes, except perhaps insuring a fair fight when two men had it out with fists. As this area, as well as all of Newfoundland, lived through much of its history as a society which did not officially exist in the eyes of the crown, and consequently there was little if any political authority ever present, you would expect that internal mechanisms would develop to maintain harmony.

Harmony, or at least lack of conflict, is what people attempt to maintain, not as an ideal striven for but as a working arrangement in everyday life. For example, the rationales for both moral behavior and neighborly co-operation are pragmatic. People maintain that it would not pay for anyone to steal because in so small a community all would know who did it, and if you do not help people when they need assistance you will not receive it when you require it yourself. These views indicate that the individual sees himself instrumentally in his social milieu. He is an adaptive agent, and helping others and not being immoral are ways in which he can maintain an optimum social position.

One way in which to maintain this state is by being "tolerant" of the excesses of others. Tolerant is not a suitable term because it implies a conscious attempt, and being able to ignore abuse in the Straits ranges from unconscious stoicism to effortful suppression. The most frequently occurring example of this is to be found in every day interaction. When two men are conversing and one is forcefully asserting some point of monopolizing the conversation, the other will remain impassive and relatively silent, only murmering, "Yes, boy," periodically in assent. When men are gathered together in the merchant's shop or in a house, and there is no drinking going on, each maintains reserve which is punctuated by a wry comment, an assertion, or a bit of news. The prevalent pattern is that of maintaining somewhat of an impassive front which serves as a buffer against the aggressions and assertions of others. At the same time when you yourself are assertive or aggressive the impassiveness of others protects them and prevents the interaction from growing into conflict.

This type of give-and-take typifies social interaction in the area. In terms of its usefulness in avoiding conflict it is said that trouble starts when one man says something abusive to another and that man cannot "let it go." He then retorts and the conflict begins. The best thing is to ignore abuse. This attitude permeates social life-- it is best to ignore irritations and avoid overt conflict. For example, if families suffer the mischief of their neighbors' children they never report this to the parents. If a man owes another money, perhaps for having bought something from him and not having the cash to pay him at the time, the creditor will go a long time without dunning the debtor, so long that when the encounter does arise enough hostility will have been built up to make it unpleasant.

If a man is being tormented or abused it is best if he "heaves it off and goes on." Most people feel that the man who ignores abuse rather than be irritated by it is the "better man," and will respect him for it.[2] Even if a man were to fight and win, his security might be affected as he might become known as a person willing to fight, and anyone looking for trouble would seek him out. Thus, if being abused it is best to either leave or ignore the irritating party and only talk to the others present.

Some men are able to endure a good deal of teasing and tormenting without it disturbing their self-possession, and they are respected. Some people can be tormenting and "keep at" a person in such a subtle way that one hardly knows they are doing it, and, of course, there is a fine line between what is serious and what is ostensibly jest.

Tolerance and self-possession are two sides of the same behavioral coin. The individual puts up with the excesses of others by erecting a barrier of impassivity. If it were not for this defense the hostility and competition of the small community would be debilitating. By "utilizing" the devices of self-possession and tolerance the individual is able to remain sufficiently uninvolved to pursue his own ends in an intimate society with a minimum of conflict. Minor breeches of the taciturn are not overtly recognized and are, therefore, not disruptive. Individuals tend to agree with direct statements as a matter of course, and an attitude of consensus is most often overtly maintained--even though it is sure that this is not the case in actuality.

Such a mechanism is a local manifestation of a general social process described by Goffman:

> When we allow that the individual projects a
> definition of the situation when he appears before
> others, we must also see that the others, however
> passive their role may seem to be, will themselves
> effectively project a definition of the situation
> by virtue of their response to the individual and
> by virtue of any lines of action they initiate to
> him. Ordinarily we find that the definitions of
> the situation projected by the several different
> participants are sufficiently attuned to one
> another so that open contradiction will not occur.
> I do not mean that there will be the kind of
> consensus that arises when each individual present
> candidly expresses what he really feels and honestly
> agrees with expressed feeling of the others present.
> This kind of harmony is an optimistic ideal and in any
> case not necessary for the smooth working of society.
> Rather, each participant is expected to suppress his
> immediate heartfelt feelings, conveying a view of the
> situation which he feels the others will be able to
> find at least temporarily acceptable. The maintenance
> of this surface of agreement, this veneer of consensus,
> is facilitated by each participant concealing his own
> wants behind statements which assert values to which
> everyone present is likely to give lip-service.
> Further, there is usually a line of division of
> definitional labour. Each participant is allowed to
> establish the tentative official ruling regarding
> matters which are vital to him but not immediately
> important to others, e.g., the rationalizations and
> justifications by which he accounts for his past
> activity; in exchange for this courtesy he remains
> silent or noncommittal on matters important to others
> but not immediately important to him. We have a kind
> of interactional _modus_ _vivendi_. Together the
> participants contribute to a single over-all definition
> of the situation which involves not so much a real agree-
> ment as to what exists but rather a real agreement as to
> whose claims concerning what issues will be temporarily
> honoured. Real agreement will also exist concerning the
> desirability of avoiding an open conflict of definitions
> of the situation. Let us refer to this level of agree-
> ment as a "working consensus." It is to be understood
> that the working consensus established in one interaction
> setting will be quite different in content from the
> working consensus established in a different type of
> setting. Thus, between two friends at lunch, a reciprocal
> show of affection, respect, and concern for the other
> is maintained. In service occupations, on the other
> hand, the specialist often maintains an image of
> disinterested involvement in the problem of the client,
> while the client responds with a show of respect for the

competence and integrity of the specialist.
Regardless of such differences in content, however,
the general form of these working arrangements is
the same (1958:3-4).

This mechanism is put under its greatest strain when men are
drinking. There is little drinking to excess during most of the year,
but during the twelve days of Christmas, seven days during Easter,
and during times and weddings there is a good deal. On the former two
occasions men go from house to house singing and stepdancing. When
they arrive at a home the host often brings forth beer or sometimes
rum, and the men of the party may stop off at the house of each in turn
so that every man has his chance as host.

These are periods of general merriment but they have their draw-
backs. Drinking for twelve days is hard physically and I have heard
men remark on how it is "a wonder" that they can keep it up. It is
also hard on the women, even though they may have only a glass or two
of wine during the period, in that they are somewhat tormented by the
men coming around who may poke through the pantry demanding food, or
play irritating pranks. This must be put up with, for to block it
would lead to bitter feelings and might mean physical violence.

Fights do sometimes develop when men have been drinking.
Hostility that has been dormant during the rest of the year now comes to
the surface as the inhibition that maintains the customary conflict
avoidance mechanism disappears. The fact that hostility that has
accumulated can be ventilated during these occasions has an adjustive
effect and no doubt compensates for the disruption caused. Fights do
not usually involve much or any injury. Men hold back the contestants
or sometimes it will be a stand off as equal numbers of men will support
each other. A few black eyes may result, but usually nothing more, and
weapons are never used. In case of a pre-arranged fight, which rarely
occurs, men supporting each contestant will be present to see that
all is fair. The day after a fight the contestants, like as not, feel
subdued and a bit foolish, and may have to bear the quiet scorn of their
wives. Such fights do not lead to feuds or to enduring hostility. After
fighting "they'll remember that they've been into a fight for about a
year, but then they'll forget about it." Even a short time after such
an affair the contestants may greet each other with cordiality in passing.

It is said that it is best not to remember anything that is said during
Christmas or Easter, "people might say anything then." These holidays,
then, plus times and weddings, are periods when hostilities engendered
are not ventilated due to the operation of normative mechanisms are
allowed expression under the guise of, and due to the effect of,
alcohol consumption. Hostilities are expressed not only because alcohol
dulls inhibitions, but also because when a man is drunk he is allowed
a great range of disruptive behavior. Such actions tend to be excused
because a person is drinking. Fighting and disruptive behavior while
under the influence of alcohol are not considered to be proper
behavior but are accepted as a part of social life.

Sometimes, when men gather to play cards they will play for drinks,
and those who win a hand can drink while the others must watch. When
men gather to drink and sing songs they often "torment" one another.
No one will sing a song until he is put upon by the others to do so.
When he sings, or indeed if he sings at all, is governed by the amount
of liquor he consumes and the prodding he receives depending, of
course, upon how inhibited he is to begin with. Most men are fairly
reticent about performing and need a bit of drink and the encouragement
of the company. After a man sings he has temporarily fulfilled his
obligation and is "off the hook." He then joins in with the others in
getting someone who has not yet performed to sing. Men will claim that
they do not know songs or have forgotten songs that are requested of
them only to sing them later when their resistance has been broken down
by the group.

If a man will not sing after much prodding he may be enjoined
to "be a man!" and his drink may be taken away, or the company may
threaten to stick him with pins if he doesn't perform. When he finally
does sing one gets the impression that he really wanted to all along
but was too shy. Singing itself can be stressful as snickers may
accompany mistakes or any pauses to recollect. When a singer finishes
he is congratulated with cries of "good boy!" indicating that such a
performance is no trivial matter.

This pattern of reticence in singing and of "passing the buck"
after the performance is illustrated by the opening and closing verses
of a local song called "The Old Crow":[3]

I'm very sorry gentlemen
You called on me to sing
For this I will offend you
I can't do any such thing
But since you called on me to sing
I'll see what I can do
And when I comes to the chorus
I hope you'll join me too
I hope you'll join me too

And now my song is ended
And I can't sing no more
My tongue is nearly worn out
My throat is getting sore
I hope I haven't offended you
Or haven't delayed you long
There's one amongst this company
Oh, _____ can sing us a song
Oh, _____ can sing us a song

Mechanisms of social regulation break down almost completely when
wrecks are stripped. The channel that comprises the Strait of Belle Isle
is narrow and long and if a ship is but little off course, it can easily
go aground in foggy weather. Although, in recent years there have been
no wrecks as radar has aided navigation.

It is felt that when the captain leaves the ship and the flag
is taken down the contents of the ship belong to anyone who takes them.
As a consequence of this, the numerous wrecks that have occurred in the
past, the daring of the local men, and local poverty, one finds many
household items that have derived from wrecks. These include tables,
wash stands, silverware, and wooden cabinets, but consumables such as
coal, lumber and food are also taken. The most famous wreck in the Strait
was that of the HMS Raleigh which went aground on Point Amour, Labrador,
directly across from Savage Cove, in August, 1922. A Newfoundland ballad
"The Northfield and the Raleigh," commemorates this wreck and that of the
Northfield which was aground on the Newfoundland side at the same time
"just nine miles apart." It is said that she was steaming north from
Port Saunders in a fog and ran aground on the Point. She was pulled over
to the Labrador side by the "down" (northeast running) tide which always
pulls towards that shore and the captain claimed that the foghorn wasn't
working. Another warship was sent to take her supplies off and after it
was through a 120 local men stripped her and divided the spoils in
equal shares. This was an exceptional situation as most wreck stripping

is chaotic.

Coping with most wrecks requires much skill and daring. A number of years ago a ship ran aground on Flower's ledges off Flower's Cove in a storm. The crew left as it was feared she would break up, and late in the night the captain did also, although he did not take down the flag. As the captain's cruiser was passed by one side of the Harbour Rock in Flower's Cove on its way in, the fishing boats were going out to the ship on the opposite side. Despite the heavy storm they stripped the ship of food, furniture, and liquor.

Wrecks inspire men with a zeal that transcends the mere acquisition of needed articles. It is each man for himself, together with those who may be helping him. Some would smash a desired article that someone else might be making off with, and the greatest danger is in getting trampled on or hit with lumber or whatever is being unloaded.[4]

Stress upon men, then, increases from normal interaction through tormenting and abusing behavior when singing and drinking, through drunkenness during periods of license to the melee of ship stripping. His ability to remain in the situation without becoming vulnerable decreases from the former through the latter as more and more stress is placed upon his defenses.

The mechanism of impassivity coupled with permissiveness is similar in function to that of the Tuareg veil as seen by Robert Murphy:

> . . . why do Tuareg males cover their faces so
> completely that only areas around the eyes and nose
> may be seen? . . . in doing so, they are symbolically
> introducing a form of distance between their selves
> and their social others. The veil, though providing
> neither isolation nor anonymity, bestows facelessness
> and the idiom of privacy upon its wearer and allows
> him to stand somewhat aloof from the perils of social
> interaction while remaining a part of it (1964:1257).

In the Straits "the veil" is the reserve and lack of commitment to a position which might be in conflict with what is being presented as opinion or attitude. Such a mechanism also allows an individual to proceed with his own plans and activities without becoming enmeshed in those of others.

> . . . the expression of distance in one form or
> another promotes autonomy of action (cf. Merton,1957:
> 375) . . . the actor allows the other enough cues so
> that the game may go on, but withholds sufficient
> stimuli so that his further course of action cannot
> be fully predicted. This not only gives him flexi-
> bility, but by decreasing the show of emotional
> attachment to the means and also the end of action he
> is not trapped into commitment. More simply, and
> elegantly, this is what is known as "playing it cool"
> (Murphy, 1964:1259).

Please note that the reserve we have been discussing is not
aloofness, which is part of the Tuareg pose. The men of the Straits
love visiting and conversation, and comraderie and joviality are almost
always present at gatherings. Nonetheless, a certain element of reserve
is always present, particularly between men who are not members of the
same crew. This can also be seen in children as shyness displayed
toward adults that they do not know well—the gaze is towards the
ground, there is reticence regarding speech, giggling, and sometimes
blushing. Men in shops will sometimes turn their backs on the stranger
and gaze out the window. All of these habits, from the most obviously
embarrassed child to the most friendly but reserved adult, serve as a
barrier behind which the individual may hide.

This lack of commitment fits in well with the competition and
individualism that one finds in the Straits. Men vie with each other
for distinctions of all types from seeing who has caught the most rabbits
to who can walk to the company camp the fastest.

> Men are always competing with each other in terms
> of who gets the most fish, rabbits, game, and almost
> anything else that they do. When they used to walk
> into the woods to the company camps they would try to
> see who could walk the fastest, and you'd be loaded
> down with gear so it was hard. And if you were slow
> by the time you got there they'd be boilin' they kettle
> and they'd say, "Ah, we beat you!"

Individuals within a crew will often compete with each other to
see who jigs the most fish, and crews will compete amongst each other for
the most fish caught in a trip or in tucking a trap. When a crew comes
in after jigging or tucking there will be inquiries from members of
other crews as to the amount of the catch, and sometimes a bit of
taunting by those who have done better.

> . . . you might challenge someone in your crew
> to see who can jig the most fish. If you get more
> than the other fellow it makes you feel better and
> it makes him feel a little bad.

Such competition is to an extent a matter of relative accomplishment.
If, for example, a man were to return from rabbit catching and encounter
a number of men who had also been at the same task, found out that he had
done worse than all of them, he would still feel good after encountering
only one individual who he had beaten. However, absolute accomplishments
are most important for prestige purposes and some men have reputations as
"big fish killers," or were "big choppers" when the company camps were
operating.

Some families feel competitive about the school grades that their
children receive. They are quite conscious of the class positions of
their children, and this motivates them to encourage their children to
do well.

Lying serves as a displacement for competition. Men often tell
exaggerated tales of their accomplishments, but they are told ostensibly
for fun. It is assumed that when a man openly tells a story that is not
believable he is telling it as a joke and that it will be accepted as
such by everyone. The teller will at some point ask someone present to
confirm the tale, and whoever is asked will automatically respond with
"Yes, boy."

In many instances the tale told is so outlandish that there
is no doubt about its being fabricated. An example is the shooting and
gastonomic abilities of one Ace Wentzel. The first of the following
paragraphs was related by one man and the second was told immediately
after by another present who seemingly wanted to out do the first.

> I heard a lot about Ace Wentzel. He was a
> wonderful gunner. If a bird rised out of a pond
> and he had a forty-four or a 30-30 on his arm,
> he would ask you if you want that bird, and if
> you said yes he'd just fire and kill the bird.

> He was a wonderful gunner but he was a wonder-
> ful hand at eating beaver, too. I laughed myself
> one time, I'll never forget it. Ace Wentzel he
> was buying furs that time for old Angus Genge, you
> know. He was at that for four or five years, and
> I said, "I'll bet you had some good scoffs" [meals
> of fresh meat]. "Now," he said, "do you know, I

had some good scoffs, but not enough." But he said,
"One time I got a big middler" [middle-sized beaver],
and, he said, "I cooked 'n and I ate every cursed
bit of 'n myself at one time." And I said, "You didn't
do that." "Yes, I did," he said.

Another example is provided by a very old man now blind living
in a neighboring settlement who once, when he thought he was entertaining
the welfare officer, told the most exaggerated stories about filling a
punt completely full with turrs during a hunting trip. His wife tried
unsuccessfully to subtly inform him that he was actually entertaining
the minister, but the old man didn't understand and after the guest
left and he discovered his error he felt quite ashamed. As there is a
strong sanction against it in the area, lying is able to proceed
because when an obvious lie is told it is assumed to be a joke. The
term lie locally covers deliberate untruth and unintentional
misinformation. Although people, of course, differentiate between the
two categories, there is a tendency to associate the latter with the
former and they will say that they did not mean to lie after having
discovered that they have unintentionally misinformed. Fiction is
considered to be lies and some parents frown on their children reading
it or listening to fairy tales.

In cases where related accomplishments are a bit out of the
ordinary, but not preposterous, the listener judges the statements on the
basis of what he knows is usually done and what can be done, and also the
known capabilities of the particular individual, for there are certain
men who are known to be outstanding in some of their activities.

It does happen, sometimes, that a man will tell a lie for fun and
someone present believes him. That man then tells someone else what he
has heard as a fact. After the third person finds out that what he has
been told is not true he calls the second person a liar. If a man gets,
say, an exceptionally large number of birds he might not be believed
unless he shows them. Sometimes a man might claim that he did less than
was actually the case, as when he finds a particular area rich in rabbits
and says that he had done poorly to keep others away.

It might be, also, that a man would rarely tell a lie about his
accomplishments that he consciously wanted people to believe, but no
matter if intended as a joke or as a deliberate misrepresentation, the lie

achieves the same end, the heightening of the prestige of the teller
in his own eyes. Telling an exaggerated story is a displacement device
for feelings of competition. It is a mock competition wherein the teller
gets some satisfaction of accomplishment (ostensibly the satisfaction of
telling a tall one) from an event which never occurred.

The interaction in which the lie is told is the same as that
described before. The tale is received with ostensible acceptance no
matter how unbelievable and people will assent to its truth if requested.
Because of this the listener is not committed to show whether he believes
or not as he hides behind a passive show of supposed acceptance, and the
teller, consequently, is not challenged or questioned.

The same pose of tolerance and reserve is used by fathers toward
their children. The youngest child is doted on and pampered, but after
being displaced by a younger sibling is to a certain extent ignored by
the father. Children can create much confusion and noise without it
perturbing adults, and fathers and mothers can be badgered by their off-
spring only to reprimand them after great provocation. Despite this
permissiveness the father maintains firm authority over the children,
even though this is rarely firmly put into effect. Mothers, by and large,
have less authority over their children than the father, but do not have
the advantage of distance and as great a threat of potential punishment.
In some households children are more indulged and cajoled than in others,
while one may also find them admonished to obey and sometimes "threatened"
when they are disobedient. Threatening consists of sternly addressing
the culprits sometimes with threats of punishment ("I'll get the cat-o-nine
after you"), but much more often children are frightened by their being
told that a stranger or someone else, real or imagined, will carry them
off if they disobey.

Some of the indifference that individuals may show to the
distractions and minor irritations of others about them is related to life
in large households of physical and emotional intimacy. This has the
effect of insulating the individual from distraction and offering him
some privacy in an intensely public communal life.

An avoidance of directness and a lack of commitment are also
mechanisms which operate to avoid embarrassing confrontation in relationship
In such techniques, again, lack of explicitness is a form of tolerance, here

of ambiguity, coupled with self-possession in terms of not stating
intentions. Such avoidance of directness takes place when an individual
wishes a favor. Without asking directly for whatever it is that is
desired to be done the desirer is able to present the subject in such a
tangential, but yet obvious manner, that although nothing is actually
requested there is no doubt as to what is desired.

As no explicit request was made, not complying does not overtly
jeopardize relations, as the person "asked" does not refuse, and the
person "asking" has not literally asked.

An example of this concerns a man from Notre Dame Bay who came
through before fishing season one year looking for a berth as a shareman. He stopped in to see a man who he heard was looking for one. There
was no doubt that he was an experienced hand, but the man who needed the
shareman didn't want to take him on as he was a stranger ("and you don't
know what he might be like") and he wanted some time off during the
season. He "never gave him the sign" that he would take him on, even
though the man kept hinting. Finally, the outsider left saying that he
would "think it over," even though nothing had been offered. Not only
was the non-committal attitude taken realistically as a refusal, but the
petitioner found it necessary to pretend that the situation was open to
avoid the possibility of any bad feeling. Similarly, there is a tendency
not to ask direct questions and correspondingly a tendency to reply to
the latter with rather vague answers.

There are other practices which prevent requests from being
disruptive. For instance, a person must sit awhile after coming in to
make a request before it is actually made. Here the idea is that the
personal relationship between solicitor and solicited is not endangered
by the idea that all that is of consequence in the visit is what is
solicited.

On the other hand when the little girl who lives next door comes
around to sell the weekly newspaper she knocks on the door even though
she walks in without knocking at all other times.[5] In doing so she puts
herself in a formal "stranger" role so that the outcome of the business
transaction will not affect the personal relationship. This is the
reverse of the technique of the urban door-to-door salesman who often
attempts to become as personal as possible in order to intimidate the

householder.

In the case of the solicitor who sits a while before making a request and the newspaper seller who knocks we have one custom which ensures intimacy and another which establishes impersonality, but both have the same function.

There are other practices which are considered good manners and which stress the maintaining of personal relationships in contrast with utilitarian ends. It is not polite to leave the house when one has guests without enjoining them to remain in one's absence. When guests go to leave they are reminded that there is "plenty of time" and enjoined to stay.

If neighbors are in the house at night when lunch is to be served they will be asked to join and people from outside the community are asked to any meal. In the latter case it is considered proper for the guest to refuse the first time asked. This custom was utilized by one man in an isolated community in the area to torment his guests. As mentioned previously in travelling one puts in at the homes of relatives, friends, or any house in lieu of the latter for food and lodging. For the most part there are no commercial alternatives for this hospitality and so the guest is quite dependent upon his host. When travellers stopped in at the house of the man in question he would offer them food and they would refuse, according to expectation, assuming that they would be asked again. He would not offer again and reputedly enjoyed watching them suffer.

Just as tolerance plus reserve serves personal ends and social tranquility by ameliorating interpersonal relationships, so co-operation maintains an individual's "social capital" among his neighbors. By helping when called upon he insures not only that he will receive aid when needed, but also that he maintains his general esteem in the community This does not mean that when a man aids a neighbor in launching a boat the neighbor has incurred an explicit obligation to help him launch his boat or perform some other particular service, but that in general being cooperative means that one will be aided when in need.

We are considering here what might be called non-contractual, rather than contractual aid. Contractual aid is manifested between crew members and in a situation where, let us say, men who are not crew

members enter into a cooperative venture such as going hunting birds
together. Each receives an equal share in the game, expenses (such as
gasoline) are equally divided, and usually no charge is made for the
use of capital equipment (such as a boat) which is furnished by one of
the parties. Such types of relationships were further discussed in
Chapter III.

Non-contractual aid obtains in situations where an individual
is called upon to contribute his time, energy or materials but does not
receive a direct share in the outcome of the effort. Examples of
this include lending of equipment, helping to launch boats, and helping
haul houses.[6] Non-contractual aid concerns situations in which a person
alone cannot be expected to cope. Everyone cannot have on hand all those
items and tools required in the various endeavors carried on by the men,
and no one man, and no single crew, can haul a house or launch a boat.

When the fishing is over motor boats are shored up on land by
placing sticks under their gunwals. The smaller boats (outboards,
punts, and flats) are usually brought ashore and turned over. These can
be carried back by the crew itself, except for the outboards which would
require a few more hands than the usual crew. The motor boats, due to
their size, require a good many men to bring them out of the water and
launch them.

In launching a boat the crew contacts other men in the community
for their aid. Only men from the settlement are asked, and in Savage
Cove usually only men from the particular side are involved, but men
from the south side will come and help on the north when asked, as they
have been when the crew with the larger boats has needed help.

The boats are brought down to the water from the beach by placing
sticks perpendicularly under the keel and sliding them along. The
keel may also be slid in the trough of a long grooved runner. There
are two of these and as the boat is slid along one, the other is placed
in front of it to receive the boat next. In both cases the boat is
supported and pushed along by a row of men on either side. There are
songs which are sung "to get everybody to haul together and to the one
swing." They are sung out by the men who all heave together on the
"haul" of the song. This insures co-ordination as "everybody hauls
at the one time and it makes it stronger, whereas if you wouldn't sing,

that one feller be haulin' and the other feller wouldn't." Two such
tunes sung in Savage Cove are "Haul on the Bowline," and "It's, Oh,
my Jolly Poker."

> Haul on the bowline
> Haul and burst the towline
> Haul on the bowline
> Haul boys, haul
>
> Oh, my jolly poker
> We shall rock and roll 'er over[7]
> And 'tis, oh, me jolly poker
> Haul

It is not uncommon for entire houses to be moved. Many men,
80 to 100, are needed for this and so it is necessary for the mover to
visit a number of settlements to invite the requisite number. No one who
comes is paid and no direct reciprocal obligation is incurred. Houses
are moved in the winter and spring so that they may be taken over the
ice. The house is slid along on two poles each of which has a rope
attached to it by means of holes at the front ends. These are cut with
an upward slanting edge so as to achieve a runner-like effect on the ice.
There is also a rope going around the back of the house itself and the
various ropes are made into two lines which are pulled by the men in
two columns.[8]

Houses are moved long distances in this manner. There is one in
Savage Cove that was moved from Nameless Cove, two miles away as the
crow flies, but much further in terms of distance traversed as the house
had to be moved along the cove and out around Yankee Point and deep
into Savage Cove. The operation took three days. There was one man in
Savage Cove who had his house moved three times between the south side
and Cooper Island. People were discouraged with helping him after the
third move, and he probably would have had difficulty getting help for
a fourth.

On a few occasions snowmobiles have fallen through the ice and
men have come together to pull them out. Men are quite willing to help
push cars stuck in the snow and in doing so they display a zeal and a
joy in the effort which transcends the mere end of extricating the
vehicle.

Occasionally fire will strike a family. The houses are of wood
and the kerosene lamps, the combustibles, including kerosene used in the
stove, and clothes drying near the stove all make for a fire hazard.
When a family loses its home in this way a collection is usually taken
by someone in the settlement who will visit the other communities as
well. Several years ago, after a fire took the lives of most of the
members of one family in Savage Cove, the other members of the community
helped the survivors to build a new house and supplied them with
furniture and household utensils.

Competition in the Straits raises the question of how a
competitive but intimate society is integrated.[9] In the Straits the
problem of social relationship is the carrying on of competition without
interrupting permanent intimate relationships. Individuals must be
able to proceed with their own plans without interfering with those
of anyone else and without isolating themselves or divorcing themselves
from the community. At the same time they must be able to cooperate
without involving themselves in incumbering alliances.

Thus, competition operating in terms of a small local society
of stable memberships presents a different picture than competition in
a fragmented urban society where the individual may have to join and
conform to the standards of groups in order to further his own ends
(Hsu, 1961:219-20).

As we have seen life in the Straits there is much comraderie,
warmth and intimacy, and little overt hostility, but at the same time
there is competition and each man goes his own way to maximize his own
endeavors. This latter does not conflict with his participation in the
extended family operation as this is a means by which he furthers his own
end. When the members do not feel it does this they will split up.
The integration of local society consists, then, of a balance between
two analytic[10] aspects of social life: individuality and group
orientation.

Three examples of such individualism will suffice. After a
snow fall has covered the only well that does not freeze in winter,
people hold out as long as possible with the water supply they have on
hand hoping that someone else will run out first so that they will have
to dig it out.

However, this situation is not without humorous and competitive aspects. He who runs out first and does the labor is roughly in the same position as the man who got the least rabbits.

A man will refrain from asking another how to do a particular thing even when it would be profitable for him to do so because in asking he would feel he would make himself appear inadequate. Of course, it is often possible to obtain the knowledge indirectly, but it does happen that men will continue to operate in an inefficient manner rather than consult someone who could supply them with a more efficient technique. Conversely, it is not good form to presume to tell someone a better way to do a thing, thus implying that his lack of knowledge is an inadequacy. It is significant that a boy becomes a man when he is able enough to do a man's work and knows the various techniques.

Another example is to be found in the individual contractual relationships that men pursue. I happened to mention that a certain man had said that he would make me a pair of racquets in front of his brother and his cousin. His cousin then said that he was making a pair for him, and not for me, as (the cousin) he in return was going to loan him his dogs to haul some wood. His brother then said that it was he that the racquets were being made for, and not the cousin, as the wood in question had already been hauled, although the cousin did not know it. This is an extreme situation, but does illustrate that even among closely linked members of a small intimate community each man goes his own way making his own commitments. Such a balance is furthered by the mechanisms we have been discussing: a wide tolerance coupled with reserve and cooperation without permanent involvement. However, there are other factors in local life which make for the same end.

One of these is the displacement of hostility outside the group. This permits aggression engendered in being tolerant to be dissipated. Such displacements occur as fear of strangers and other fantasy figures (Firestone, n.d.) and fear of ghosts which was widespread a generation ago. Hostility also is manifested in other ways. Children continuously throw rocks at birds, and at each other, and sled dogs are feared and distrusted. The term[fish killer][fisherman] is perhaps significant in this regard.

Also, as there is no local government, almost no formal cooperation
is necessary. The only non-church organization in the area is the Orange
Lodge which is not very active and there are no members in Savage Cove.
The schools are church run and the local woman's group, the C.E.W.A.,
is an Anglican organization. Two men serve as church members for the
local church. They act as ushers and are responsible for the upkeep
of the structure. There are two school board members who together with
the members from the other settlements form the mission board and are
in charge of the local school building. The men of the community take
turns "putting in" the fire in the school house in the morning and the
women take turns cleaning it.

The settlement is allotted two dollars per head by the government
for road work. During the last two years this money has been used to hire
the highway department crews who with their equipment have extended the
communities roads. However, before this, the money went to pay those men
of the community who wished to work on the roads. To facilitate this
there are two men who act as foreman and time keeper.

Talk and conversation, and, of course, gossip articulate men's
activities with those of others. A place where much of this is done is
in the house that serves as the unofficial meeting place of the men of
the community. They drop over to this house after supper on weekdays
and also after dinner on Sundays. The only women present are those of
the household. Here "the news" is discussed and the activities and
plans of the area mulled over. Much of the congregating is motivated by
the need for male companionship and one finds that men who are not
associated with large crews are the more consistent participants.

If one takes to heart such conceptions as Gemeinschaft-
Gesellchaft (Toennies, 1935) and the "Folk-Urban Continuum" (Redfield,
1941) there is the danger of feeling that a folk society should manifest
such characteristics as John Messenger cites as examples of a "primitivist"
view.

> . . .folk societies possess simple, statis
> cultures in which dysfunctional forms are rare;
> their economies are primarily subsistence ones,
> approximate the householding types, and lack
> competitive elements [italics mine]; political
> structures are mostly informal; the family is the
> core social group and is a highly integrated,

> cooperative unit; religion is a pervasive force
> that sanctions all behavior and assures psychological
> security and social cohesion; and, religious dissent
> and skepticism are unknown. Primitivists also hold
> that folk people are content with their conditions
> of life, are seldom if ever mentally ill, and
> exhibit character traits that civilization has
> tended to pervert (1964:16).

Such an orientation would, I presume, equate a static and harmonious existence to, at least in part, a lack of competition. However, in the Straits one finds both competition and a relatively harmonious way of life in settlements in which interaction is intimate and the ethos egalitarian.

If one were to go by the previously mentioned conceptions it might be thought that what exists in the Straits is a combination of antithetical elements, but this would be a misinterpretation.

FOOTNOTES TO CHAPTER I

1. "Steady - that part of a river which widens until there is no perceptible current" (Story, 1959:69).

2. ". . . Anchor Point (the cape at the base of which the settlement is situated) . . . marks the southwest entrance to the Straits of Belle Isle . . ." (James, 1937:51).

3. Not to be confused with the settlement of Eddies Cove West, 55 miles to the southeast.

4. Pronounced karpoon (rhymes with harpoon).

5. To be exact, the Strait Coast ran from West Point, just southwest of Eddies Cove, to East Point, southwest of Open Bay, which is just southwest of Boat Harbour (Seary, 1960:35).

6. Local name (Savage Cove) is Green Island.

7. This same situation is to be found in other parts of Newfoundland.

    " . . . the ridge on the south-east side of the (St. John's) harbor, which, from the people all using compass bearings instead of true, is called the south side, and the ridge the south side hill."

    " . . . the western (or as it is called in Newfoundland the northern) shore of Conception Bay" (Jukes, 1842:I, 41).

    "'The western shore' in the parlance of the east coast fishermen means any part of the south and west coasts from Placentia Bay to the southern part of the Straits of Belle Isle" (James, 1937:I, 51).

8. "Modern maps show variously Flower, Flowers, Flower's" (Seary, 1960:52).

9. This is called Pines Cove locally. The highway sign says "Pines Cove."

10. Unless otherwise indicated, place names used are those which occur on the National Topographic Series maps (in case there are differing local names, or local names which do not occur on the maps).

11. "A tickle is a passage between an island and the mainland, or between two islands" (James, 1937:59).

12. The road which connects the settlements is called the highroad. Each settlement has its own "branch."

138

FOOTNOTES TO CHAPTER II

1. In fact G. O. Rothney (1964:3) states, "Before Columbus sailed in
   1492, and most probably in 1481, Englishmen from Bristol
   discovered Newfoundland. They called it 'Brazil,' the name of
   an imaginary island on late medieval maps."

2. That he was the leader seems to be contradicted by Richards'
   statement that after "Robert Bartlett, an old man with plenty of
   means, returned to England where he died . . . Robert Genge . . .
   a great furrier . . . stayed on as head man on Anchor Point room,
   until he dies of old age" (1953a:18).

3. Originally spelled Cowles (Mission of the Straits of Belle Isle
   1849-. Hereafter abbreviated as M.S.B.I.).

4. These first names assumed on the basis of M.S.B.I.

5. Known locally then, and until the last generation as Poverty Cove.
   It sometimes appears in the Mission register as Sandy Bay
   (M.S.B.I.).

6. However, regarding his nationality, Richard later (1853a:20) states,
   "Big William when he grew old went back to Jersey . . ."

7. The great summer migrations of floaters and stationers from eastern
   Newfoundland to the Labrador were a result of the Newfoundlanders
   being prohibited from fishing on the French Shore (MacKay, 1946:27).

8. Unless otherwise specified, historical material from the beginning
   of the chapter to this point is derived from Richards (1953a,
   1953b).

9. For instance in Historic Newfoundland (English, n.d.:60),
   " . . . it is not all difficult to appreciate the depths of dispair
   of those who experience hardships or disaster on the rugged coastline. They gave to us such place names as: . . .

10. See Chapter I, page 3.

11. On "A map of the North Atlantic by Le Bocage Boissaie, 'Idrographe
    et Professeur Roial en la nauigation du haure de grace,' 1669.
    A copy of the map is in the Depot Hydrographique de la Marine,
    Paris" (Seary, 1959:30).

12. Mr. Gaulton's illiteracy seems atypical, as most of the men who
    settled the area could write, or at least sign their names, in
    contrast with their offspring who had not the opportunity of
    education. The signatures of the former can be seen on marriage
    certificates in the church records (M.S.B.I.) in contrast with
    the marks, "A's" of their progeny.

13. The term Straits will be used to designate a social area comprising communities both up and down the coast from Savage Cove. The term Strait, or Strait of Belle Isle, will be used in a strictly geographical sense.

14. This is generally true of Newfoundland. The only inland towns, such as Deer Lake, Gander, and Grand Falls, are quite recent.

15. From Jacques-a-tierre, jack ashore.

16. There are minor dialect variations within the social area, even between adjacent settlements.

17. Although people tell of one neighboring community where in the past some of the inhabitants would bar their doors when strangers were around. Insofar as strangers are feared, but still are dealt with well, the latent functions of this disquieting belief can be operative without much interferring with social action (see below).

18. For a more involved analysis of the relationship between strangers and these other figures, and the latent functions of attitudes toward them, see, "Mummers and Strangers in Northern Newfoundland" (Firestone, n.d.).

19. Times can only be held on a weekend night because school is in session during the week. They cannot be held on Saturday night because Sabbath taboos would necessitate their ending at midnight and prohibit cleaning the school on Sunday.

20. Even cows are addressed as maid. This would be the equivalent of their being called girl in the United States.

FOOTNOTES TO CHAPTER III

1. These terms may also be used to refer to the men of an entire community, as, say, the "Sandy Cove crew," or any other group of men.

2. Strangers are also addressed as skipper. The various meanings of this term reflect, I feel, not so much derivations from a primary meaning as a generic terminology indicating "male leader-respected person."

3. The term company may refer to any group of men collected for a particular purpose or a group of animals as in "a company of ducks."

4. Many of the old houses were made from lumber that was hand sawed from pine balk which was presumably washed ashore having been lost overboard off schooners. There is no suitable timber in the area which might have provided it. Planks were cut from these timbers by pit sawing. One of the operators stood in a pit or on the floor of a store while the other stood above ground or in the loft of the store. As the saw was hauled back and forth across the pit opening or the hole in the loft it cut the timber that was being pushed along the ground or the floor of the loft.

5. If the orphaned son splits with his uncle and cousins upon acquiring his share, we would have a three generation extended family. If he remains with them it would be a four generation extended family.

6. This is also done in a settlement in the northeast of Newfoundland studied by James Faris (personal communication).

7. These social groups are patrilocal extended families rather than descent groups of any type because they contain no "unilinear rule of descent as an integral factor in the structure of the group." If there were such a rule we would have according to Murdock's classification, structure somewhat like patri-clans (Murdock, 1949: 66), as after marriage women tend to become affiliated with their husband's groups. "A compromise kin group [clan] is commonly larger than an extended family, but the alignment of kinsmen is identical. The principal distinction is the addition of a unilineal rule of descent as an integral factor in the structure of the group. The core of a unilocal extended family always consists of persons of one sex who are in fact unilinearly related, but this relationship is purely incidental, need not be formulated, and is frequently not even recognized. The bond of union is primarily and often exclusively residential. In a compromise kin group, on the other hand, the unilinear relationship of the core of the group is at least as crucial an integrating fact as the residential alignment" (1949:66).

8. An exception to this is Sandy Cove where many of the older houses were built with their backs towards the sea.

9. This "tipi" of sticks is built around three <u>shear sticks</u> which are placed triangularly in the ground with their tops tied together. Shear sticks are also used as a support around which hay pooks [stacks] are made.

10. I have been told by outsiders working in Harrington Harbor (an English speaking settlement on Harrington Island about 100 miles southwest of Savage Cove off the Quebec coast) that at wedding teas guests are invited to particular "settings."

11. The Mission of the Strait of Belle Isle included both sides of the Straits with headquarters at Forteau. The present mission for the Newfoundland shore is the Anglican Mission of Flower's Cove.

12. Of course, in order to fully pursue this point one would need to know something of the history and distribution of shares in fishing boats and particularly if English and Irish fishermen have co-operating families in which men have shares.

FOOTNOTES TO CHAPTER IV

1. Not to be confused with jiggers which are sometimes formally referred to as handlines.

2. Long pieces of wood or lumber or the trunks of trees are <u>sticks</u>, <u>splits</u> are small pieces of wood used for starting fires.

3. As Wise gives no averages for these factors it was necessary to divide totals from his Table XXXII, "Breakdown of Non-Cash Income of Fisherman's Families," by 35, the number of heads of households polled.

FOOTNOTES TO CHAPTER V

1. There are situations, such as the Thirty Years War or feuding in some societies which is almost continuous, in which disruption becomes almost constant. However, even in such situations accommodation is made: on the one hand perhaps in the fatalistic style of Brecht's, Mother Courage, and on the other, in the various regulative rules that apply in Riff feuding.

2. The phrase the better man is also used to indicate the winner of a fight. Likewise, if a man felt quite confident that he was the better man in this sense he might be tempted to fight.

3. The plot of this song concerns a man who courts a cook. As she is feeding him in her kitchen the master of the house comes home unexpectedly. The suitor hides in the chimney, but after a fire has been built in it the butter that the cook has put in his pockets drips, causing the fire to blaze, and he is detected. The master finally drives him out by pouring water down the flue and "he is obliged to bundle out" black as an old crow.

4. Regarding the excitement and competition engendered in stripping wrecks on the Cornwall coast Jenkin relates an incident wherein the remains of an airplane were stripped.

"By one o'clock in the morning, practically the whole population of the town was assembled on the beach, anxiously awaiting the going down of the tide. Foremost among the crowd were a number of visitors who corrupted, no doubt by the Cornish element amongst which they found themselves, nevertheless showed surprising acumen in seizing many of the most valuable portions of the wreck once the looting began! One remembers in particular a clock which was one of the most coveted of the spoils and which went to an upcountry visitor, despite the efforts of a local fisherman who was heard to remark afterwards: 'Ais, I had my eye on that, too, but darn'ee, the London fellow was too quick. Anyone would think he'd been a wrecker all his days!'"

"Most people, indeed, have only to experience for themselves the white heat of excitement which the circumstances of a wreck breeds, in order to understand how the Cornishman's reputation in this respect was gained. On such occasions, the most prosaic and respectable people will often reveal a predatory instinct of which they themselves were previously quite unconscious, and in the darkness of the night, with the sound of the breaking surf, and the ringing of the gale in one's ears, old instincts and devils will awake to life again in a most surprising way" (1945:42-43).

5. I am grateful to James Faris for pointing out this behavior to me. It also occurs in the Newfoundland community in which he worked.

144

6. Contractual aid and non-contractual aid are but ideal types. In non-contractual situations there is an investment for eventual reward, and in some instances, as in helping a man cut wood for a boat he is building, the implication is that he will have some claim on the use of the boat.

7. This line is sometimes sung, "We shall roll the bastard over."

8. Pictures of this are to be found in Greenleaf (1933:340).

9. I am using the definitions of co-operation, competition, and individualistism used in Mead (1961:8, 16).

"Competition: the act of seeking or endeavoring to gain what another is endeavoring to gain at the same time."

"Cooperation: the act of working together to one end."

" . . . Individualistic behavior . . . is, behavior in which the individual strives toward his goal without reference to others."

10. Analytic is used as these aspects exist only from the point of view of comparatively based outside observation.

BIBLIOGRAPHY

ARENSBERG, CONRAD M.

1937   The Irish Countryman. New York, Macmillan.

CENSUS OF CANADA, 1961

1961   Bureau of Statistics. Ottawa.

CENSUS OF NEWFOUNDLAND AND LABRADOR, 1935

1937   Department of Public Health and Welfare. St. John's.

CHIARAMONTE, LOUIS

n.d.   "The Relationship of Indirectness to Deep Harbour Value
Orientation." Ms.

COPES, PARZIVAL

1961   St. John's and Newfoundland - an Economic Survey. St. John's,
Newfoundland Board of Trade.

ENGLISH, L. E. F.

n.d.   "Historic Newfoundland." St. John's, Newfoundland Tourist
Development Division of the Department of Economic Development.

FARIS, JAMES C.

1966   Cat Harbour: A Newfoundland Fishing Settlement. Newfoundland
Social and Economic Studies No. 3, Institute of Social and Economic
Research, Memorial University of Newfoundland, St. John's.

FIRESTONE, MELVIN M.

n.d.   "Mummers and Strangers in Northern Newfoundland." A paper
presented before the 1964 meeting of the American Association of
the Advancement of Science.

FRANKENBERG, RONALD

n.d.   "British Community Studies." Ms.

GOFFMAN, ERVING

1959   The Presentation of Self in Everyday Life. Garden City,
Doubleday.

GREENLEAF, ELISABETH BRISTAL and GRACE YARROW MANSFIELD

1933   Ballads and Sea Songs of Newfoundland. Cambridge, Harvard
University Press.

HARE, F. KENNETH

1952 "The Climate of Newfoundland, a Geographical Analysis."
Geographical Bulletin, No. 2:36-88.

1956 "The Position of Certain Forest Boundaries in Southern
Labrador-Ungava." Geographical Bulletin, No. 8:51-73.

HEAD, C. GRANT

1963 "Community Geographical Surveys: the Northeast Coast, the
Southern Avalon, the Northern St. Barbe." St. John's, Institute
of Social and Economic Research, Memorial University of Newfoundland.

HSU, FRANCIS L. K.

1961 "American Core Value and National Character." In Psychological
Anthropology, Approaches to Culture and Personality. Homewood,
Illinois, Dorsey Press.

INGSTAD, HELGE

1964 "Vinland Ruins Prove Vikings Found the New World." National
Geographic, 126:708-34.

JAMES. M. J.

1937 "The Geography of Newfoundland." In The Book of Newfoundland,
ed. J. R. Smallwood, 2 vols. St. John's, Book Publishers.

JENKIN, A. K. HAMILTON

1945 Cornwall and Its People. London, Dent.

JUKES, JOSEPH BEETE

1942 Excursions in and About Newfoundland, During the Years 1839
and 1840 . . . 2 vols. London, John Murray.

MACKAY, R. A. ed.

1946 Newfoundland; Economic Diplomatic and Strategic Studies.
Toronto, Oxford University Press.

MEAD, MARGARET

1953 "National Character." In Anthropology Today, Sol Tax et al.,
eds. Chicago, University of Chicago Press.

1961 Cooperation and Competition among Primitive Peoples. Enlarged
edition. Boston, Beacon Press.

MESSENGER, JOHN

1964 "Man of Aran Revisited: an Anthropological Critique." A paper
presented before the American Committee for Irish Studies in 1964.

MILLS, ALAN ed., and KENNETH PEACOCK, piano accompanyment

1958 Favorite Songs of Newfoundland. Toronto, Canada Limited.

MISSION OF THE STRAIT OF BELLE ISLE (M.S.B.I.)

1849- Church records (at the parsonage, Flower's Cove).

MURDOCK, GEORGE PETER

1949 Social Structure. New York, Macmillan.

MURPHY, ROBERT F.

1964 "Social Distance and the Veil." American Anthropologist,
66:1257-1274.

NEWFOUNDLAND FISHERIES DEVELOPMENT COMMITTEE

1953 Report. St. John's.

PERLIN, A. B. , ed. and comp.

1959 The Story of Newfoundland. St. John's.

PHILBROOK, TOM

1966 Fisherman, Logger, Merchant, Miner: Social Change and
Industrialism in Three Newfoundland Communities. Newfoundland
Social and Economic Studies No. 1, Institute of Social and Economic
Research, Memorial University of Newfoundland, St. John's.

RADCLIFFE-BROWN, A. R.

1952 "The Study of Kinship Systems." In Structure and Function
in Primitive Society. Glencoe, Free Press.

REDFIELD, ROBERT

1941 The Folk Culture of Yucatan. Chicago, University of Chicago
Press.

1955 The Little Community. Chicago, University of Chicago Press.

RICHARDS, J. T.

1953a "The First Settlers on the French Shore." Newfoundland
Quarterly, vol. 3, no. 3:17-19.

1953b "The First Settlers on the French Shore" (concluded).
Newfoundland Quarterly, vol. 52, no. 4:15-16, 23.

ROTHNEY, G. O.

1964 Newfoundland, a History. Canadian Historical Association,
Historical Booklet, no. 10. Ottawa.

148

SEARY, E. R.

1959 "Toponomy of the Island of Newfoundland." Checklist, No. 1,
Sources I, Maps. St. John's, Memorial University of Newfoundland.

1960 "Toponomy of the Island of Newfoundland." Checklist, No. 2,
Names, I, The Northern Peninsula. St. John's, Memorial University
of Newfoundland.

STORY, G. M.

1959 "Newfoundland Dialect." In The Story of Newfoundland, ed. A. B.
Perlin. St. John's.

SZWED, JOHN

1966 Private Cultures and Public Imagery: Interpersonal Relations
in a Newfoundland Peasant Society. Newfoundland Social and Economic
Studies No. 2, Institute of Social and Economic Research, Memorial
University of Newfoundland, St. John's.

TOQUE, REV. PHILIP

1878 Newfoundland: As it was, and as it is in 1877. Toronto,
John B. Magrun.

TOENNIES, FERDINAND

1935 Gemeinschaft und Gesellschaft: Grundbergrife der reinen
Sociologie. Leipzig.

TUCKER, REV. H. W.

1877 Memoir of the Life and Episcopate of Edward Field, D. D.
Bishop of Newfoundland. London, Wells Gardner.

ISER BOOKS

Studies

Mailing Address:
ISER Books (Institute of Social and Economic Research)
Memorial University of Newfoundland
St. John's, Newfoundland, Canada, A1C 5S7